JAPANESE
COOKING
FOR THE SOUL

JAPANESE COOKING

FOR THE SOUL

HEALTHY

MINDFUL

DELICIOUS

1 3 5 7 9 10 8 6 4 2

Published in 2020 by Ebury Press an imprint of Ebury Publishing,
20 Vauxhall Bridge Road,
London SW1V 2SA

Ebury Press is part of the Penguin Random House group of companies
whose addresses can be found at global.penguinrandomhouse.com

Text © Hana Group UK Limited 2020
Photography © Hana Group UK Limited 2020
Illustration © Hana Group UK Limited 2020

Recipe Writer: Emma Marsden
Cover Design: Two Associates
Design: Akihiro Nakayama
Photography: Howard Shooter
Food Styling: Denise Smart
Illustrator: Max Antoine Lalande d'Anciger
Editor: Muna Reyal
Additional Recipe Testing: Angela Nilsen

Hana Group UK Limited has asserted its right to be identified as the author of this work in
accordance with the Copyright, Designs and Patents Act 1988

This edition first published by Ebury Press in 2020

www.penguin.co.uk

A CIP catalogue record for this book is available from the British Library

ISBN 9781529106077

Printed and bound in China by C&C Offset Printing Co., Ltd

Oven temperatures are for a conventional oven.
If you are using a fan oven, reduce the temperature given by 20°C.

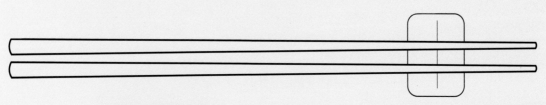

CONTENTS

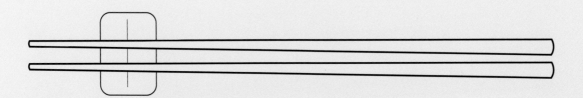

INTRODUCTION

I heard an expression in Japan that seven gods live in one grain of rice, which emphasises how important every morsel of food is and this belief is expressed in *itadakimasu*.

The heart of the *itadakimasu* ritual is one of gratitude and reflection, even if only for a moment. In its simplest form, *itadakimasu* is used before you receive something which is why the Japanese say it before they dine. You are 'receiving' heavenly food, after all and, in this light, starting a meal with *itadakimasu* implies you'll finish all of it. Something gave up its life for the meal, so it can be considered disrespectful to leave food behind. Next time you see just one last grain of rice in your bowl, don't be afraid to spend time trying to fish it out.

But the gratitude of *itadakimasu* reaches beyond the dinner table and into our everyday lives. Whatever you receive, be it an umbrella, flowers, bottle of wine or sake or a letter from a friend, receive it with appreciation, as the heart of *itadakimasu* is gratitude for the things you've been offered and a determination to make the most of what you have.

Healthy, happy and unstressed fish or animals not only taste better but offer a respect for the environment – truly the spirit of *itadakimasu*. Buying sustainable fish not only means great-tasting sushi but importantly also ensures fresh fish for future generations. We use long lines on our fishing boats to avoid dragging up the sea bed, bird 'scarers' to avoid trapping albatross and other large birds, GPS tracking to ensure we only fish in sustainable waters, and round hooks to avoid the by-catch of turtles as we care as passionately about the environment as we do about food quality.

We wonder about the longevity of Japanese island inhabitants, which is believed to be secured through a sense of community, keeping active, reducing stress and eating well. Japanese food can also be incredibly good for you.

Healthy, fresh and fun, sushi provides effortless and delicious nourishment for your body. This Japanese delicacy consists of rice, seasoned with vinegar, and is most commonly combined with fresh fish and/or vegetables. Low in saturated fats and sugars, sushi can provide a wholesome, balanced meal with a number of health benefits. Oily fish such as salmon and tuna are excellent sources of protein, selenium and omega-3 fatty acids, which are essential for the good function of the brain and cardiovascular system. In addition, research has shown that omega 3 can help improve mood and memory. Fresh vegetables such as cucumber and avocado contain a variety of essential minerals and vitamins. The seaweed, nori, is high in iodine which helps to regulate metabolism. Finally, accompanying ingredients such as ginger and wasabi are rich in antioxidants, helping to protect the skin and improve immune function.

So many amazing ingredients have been discovered in Japan, such as miso, which is made simply from soy beans, salt and often with the addition of rice or barley. Miso is made by fermenting those ingredients, turning starch into sugar. The fermentation is started by 'koji', that prized fungus grown on rice, barley or beans and the same method is used to make soy sauce or sake.

Miso is a great source of minerals and proteins and cholesterol-lowering compounds. The fermentation boosts the antioxidant levels of the soy beans (isoflavones, an antioxidant, is unique to soy beans).

A dash of soy sauce adds zest but should be used carefully so as to control your salt intake – while Japanese food can be good for you and we appreciate its flavours, part of *itadakimasu* is also in respecting the ingredients.

Despite its simplicity, the cuisine is extremely refined and varied. I have immersed myself in ramen, teppanyaki and sushi over the last three years, though I have spent most of my career in French restaurants, and I remember a Japanese chef who taught me about perfection and respect for ingredients. This appreciation that I discovered in Japanese cuisine has been profound (though I find similarities in a European kitchen, where bones would be chopped, roasted and simmered with water and vegetables to make a stock – in Japan, dried skipjack and seaweed is used to make dashi, which is also stock, but both offer deep and complex umami flavours). Some of the recipes in this book have also been influenced by other cuisines, for example, the Hawaiian poke, and the Chinese-inspired gyoza and dim sum, which have become part of Japanese food culture.

We dedicate this book to those talented chefs and to *itadakimasu* that originates from Japan's heritage in Buddhism, which teaches respect for all living things. This philosophy extends to meals in the form of thanks to the plants, animals, farmers, hunters, chefs, foragers and everything that went into the meal.

Happy cooking and happy rolling…

Jason Lalande d'Anciger
Managing Director, Hana Group UK & Ireland

OUR GUIDE TO JAPANESE INGREDIENTS

AONORI – a powdered, flaked seaweed that is often sprinkled on the outside of an inside-out roll to provide both flavour and texture. You can achieve a similar result by chopping a sheet of nori (see right) and then whizzing in a blender (it needs a very sharp blade though) to blitz the pieces more finely.

DASHI POWDER – used to flavour ramen broth, it's made from kombu (dried kelp) and dried bonito (a type of tuna) to give that unique umami savoury taste.

EEL SAUCE – this is a thick and syrupy sauce but doesn't actually contain any eel – it's associated with the fish as it's used to cover it. It's made with soy sauce (of course), sugar and a thickener. Lots of Japanese use brown sauce instead of this!

IKURA – roe from salmon that is slightly bigger than tobiko (see entry, right). Ranging from reddish orange to dark orange, this provides a pop of colour on top of the Wasabi Ebi on page 24. There's an essence of fish and salt about them with a delicate oily texture.

KIZAMI RED GINGER – a spoonful of this red/pink pickled ginger looks alluring on top of ramen and provides that all-important sweet-and-sour touch to lift a simple broth. Available in wafer-thin rounds or chopped into matchsticks.

LA-YU – this red-coloured oil is a Japanese chilli oil and is made with ground dried chillies.

MATCHA POWDER – with its bright green hue, this is reputedly packed with antioxidants and goodness. It's made by grinding down matcha green tea leaves into a very fine powder. As well as making a refreshing tea, it can also be used in baking and ice cream.

MAYU GARLIC OIL – a dark garlic oil made from cooking garlic in a neutral oil, until it turns black. This is blitzed (sometimes with sesame oil and/or salt) and used to season recipes.

MIRIN – a sweet rice wine, slightly syrupy in texture, used in stir-fries and marinades (similar to sake but lower in alcohol). You can use rice vinegar instead but mix it with caster sugar. Aged mirin is darker and looks like a dark spirit (such as whisky or brandy). Bottles labelled 'honteri', which in Japanese translates to 'like real mirin', mean that it doesn't contain any alcohol.

MISO – there are lots of variations to this soya bean paste, depending on how long it has been fermented for. Miso dare is a dark brown paste and contains just soya, salt and water. The putty or butter-coloured white miso is made with soya beans, grains (such as rice), water and salt and has a lighter flavour. Red miso has a higher proportion of soya beans to grains and gives a saltier taste.

NORI – made from algae (a type of seaweed) that is shredded and pressed together. It's used to wrap sushi rice in variations of maki. Available in half sheets ('half cut') or full sheets which can be cut in half to make the right size. It is also used as a garnish for ramen.

NERI GOMA (sesame paste) – the Japanese equivalent of tahini, but made from black sesame seeds.

PANKO BREADCRUMBS – these dried breadcrumbs have a fine texture to give good coverage and are key to creating the crisp and crunchy outer layer in chicken katsu.

RICE WINE VINEGAR – also known as rice vinegar, it's made by fermenting rice until the sugars turn into alcohol and then into vinegar. It has a mild flavour so is suitable for dips and dressings. Cider vinegar can be used instead.

SAKE (dry) – Japanese rice wine enjoyed with meals that, just like a dry white wine, can be used to cook with, too.

SEASONED VINEGAR FOR SUSHI RICE – a ready-made combination of sugar, salt and rice vinegar to season sushi rice. If you can't get hold of it, pour 3 tablespoons rice vinegar into a pan and add 2 tablespoons caster sugar and 1 teaspoon salt. Heat gently to dissolve the sugar and salt and use in the recipe.

SESAME OIL – available in pure and toasted form (the toasted tends to be slightly darker). Pure oil can be used for stir-frying as it has a higher smoke point. The toasted oil should only be used for dressings. Use both sparingly as sesame oil has a strong taste and can overpower the flavour of other ingredients.

SHAOXING RICE WINE – this caramel-coloured Chinese cooking wine is made from water, rice and wheat. Although it contains alcohol, it's used in stir-fries and other recipes. Flavour-wise, it's similar to a dry sherry, so swap for that if necessary. You may also see it labelled 'shaoshing'.

SHICHIMI POWDER – an orange seasoning made from seven spices: dried chilli, yuzu peel, Sansho (a Japanese pepper whose Latin name is *zanthxylum piperitum*), aonori and poppy, hemp and black sesame seeds. It's super spicy so you only need a small amount to give flavour.

SUSHI RICE – this short-grain, pearlised rice should be rinsed well under cold running water to remove all the starch before cooking. Once it's cooked until tender, it's seasoned with a special vinegar (see left) before using.

TAMARI SOY SAUCE – a pure soy sauce (no added ingredients), which has been fermented and has a slightly thicker texture than regular soy. It's lower in salt and will either contain less wheat or none at all so can be useful for those following a gluten-free diet.

TERIYAKI MARINADE – a thin sauce with the colour and consistency of soy sauce (one of the ingredients) and used to marinate meat, fish and tofu and for cooking sauces.

TERIYAKI SAUCE – ranges from a thin sauce to a thicker, syrupy texture. It differs from the marinade in that it is used for both cooking and is also eaten just as it is for extra flavour, for instance, over sushi. Pour into a squeezy bottle with a small nozzle to create a restaurant-style drizzle.

TOBIKO – these tiny little eggs are flying fish roe and the perfect garnish to some of our sushi or used inside to create texture and a little burst of fishy essence. We like to use the orange tobiko – a bright luminescent colour – but you can also find it in yellow or green, which have been dyed with flavourings and/or food colourings.

TOFU – made from soya, this vegan protein is now widely available in supermarkets. Silken or soft tofu has a creamy flavour, delicate texture and long shelf life and is found in small Tetra Pak boxes in the storecupboard aisle. Cut into pieces carefully and lower into broth, taking care that it doesn't break up. The firm, fresh variety is preserved in water and is found in the chilled section. It is slightly more forgiving, but should be pressed first to remove all liquid (see our tip on page 70). It can be sliced or chopped into larger chunks without breaking up, then marinated and stir-fried or deep-fried with or without a batter. Also available smoked, which has a stronger flavour.

TONKATSU PASTE – you may also find this as a sauce. Its tangy, fruity flavour can pep up a simple ramen base stock.

VIETNAMESE RICE PAPER – these stiff translucent rounds are made from water, rice and salt and are a great staple storecupboard ingredient as they last for ages. They come in several sizes so make sure you check before buying. They're very easy to use and just require a quick dip in a bowl of warm water to rehydrate before filling (see page 76).

YAKISOBA SAUCE – is a typical Japanese condiment used in noodle stir-fries. It's a fruity flavoured, slightly spiced brown sauce which is also made with a little oyster sauce (so isn't suitable in vegetarian or vegan recipes).

YUZU JUICE – the juice from the citrus fruit, yuzu, and it gives that all-important dash of mouth-puckering sourness to dressings.

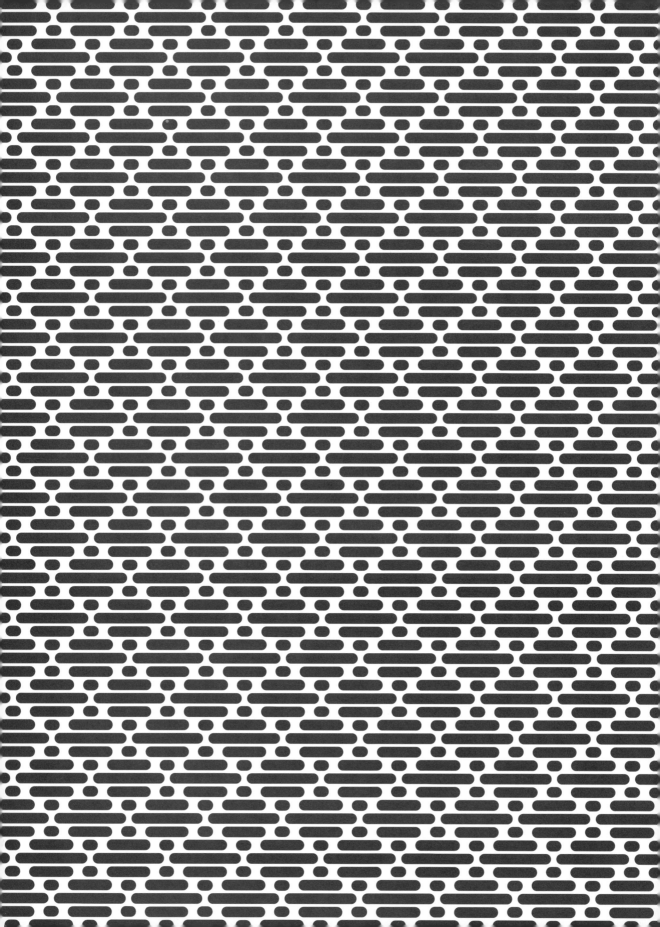

CHAPTER 1

SUSHI
&
MAKI

食わず嫌い

kuwazu girai

—

To 'dislike without eating'.

Y ou may have only recently fallen for these bite-size balls of rice wrapped in seaweed (and covered in fish or tofu) but they've been around since the late eighteenth century.

When Tokyo chefs were looking for a way to bind their hand-held rice and fish dishes, the wrapping, in the form of dried nori sheets, was created. Nori grew well and bountifully on the stakes that held the local fishermen's nets and it had been harvested for food to eat, too. But it wasn't until a paper merchant found a clever solution for the chefs by combining this fresh algae with the principles of paper-making that an edible sheet was created that could hold the two ingredients together.

It's this creation, *maki*, that's the most simple form of sushi, where the seaweed is wrapped around a vegetable and/or fish filling. If you've never made sushi before, try these recipes first. They're the easiest way to practise your rolling skills as your fingers get used to holding the ingredients on top of the rice while your thumbs and palms use the bamboo mat to move the nori to wrap around the rice. It sounds complicated as different parts of your hands are used to do separate jobs but after trying a couple of times you'll be on a roll (sorry!). Make one of the first recipes in this chapter, such as the Cucumber or Avocado Maki and you'll have a four-ingredient vegetarian lunch ready to go. Then experiment with other recipes. The Luxury Calamari Rolls, on page 36, features a home-made pickled calamari salad on top of a cucumber and avocado filling. Or try the Tuna Crunch Rolls on page 28, featuring a double-fish element of tempura prawns in the roll and a topping of sashimi tuna. Crispy fried onions sprinkled on top provide a contrasting finish.

While maki features nori on the outside, *uramaki* is an inside-out roll where the nori becomes a thin circlet of green between the rice and the filling. The sticky quality of the seasoned sushi rice is key here, as it needs to stick to the nori without falling off. Pressing it in well first helps this stage. Then once the sheet is flipped over it's ready to fill. Try, for instance, the classic California roll (see page 29) – cucumber, avocado and sashimi salmon – which can be covered either in thin slices of salmon or avocado as in our dazzling Double Salmon Roll (see page 32). Alternatively, keep it simple with an umami drizzle of spicy mayo and teriyaki sauce followed by a sprinkle of crispy fried onions.

For a big fat roll, try your hand at futomaki. You start by rolling the short end up which means the roll is thicker than the others. You don't end up with the same length of roll, so it'll cut into fewer slices.

If you're looking for something without the nori seaweed altogether, try the nigiri or cristal roll. The nigiri is an oval-shaped portion of rice covered with a slice of fish or tofu, while the cristal roll (see page 40) calls for a round of softened rice paper to encase the ingredients within.

すし飯　　　　　　　　　　　PERFECT SUSHI RICE

Great sushi starts with the perfect base of rice, one that sticks together well and holds its shape. To make it, it's important to follow a few simple steps, but there's no need for any complicated equipment – just a large bowl, a sieve and a pan with a tight-fitting lid.

Put the rice into a sieve and run cold water over the top. With the water running, use your hand to swirl through the rice until the water runs clear. This rinses the rice of any starch and dust from when the rice was milled.

Return the rice to the bowl and leave it to rest for at least 30 minutes before cooking and no more than 4 hours.

Tip the washed rice into the pan and pour over the correct quantity of cold water. You'll need 120 per cent water to the volume of rice. Don't worry about doing the maths on this – we've done that for you in each recipe. It's just useful to know if you need to cook a much bigger quantity of rice. Put a tight-fitting lid on the pan and bring to the boil. As soon as the water's boiling, turn the heat down to its lowest setting and cook for 8 minutes.

Take the pan off the heat, without lifting the lid, and leave to rest for 25–30 minutes. When the rice has finished resting, pour over the seasoned vinegar for sushi rice and use a wooden spoon or plastic spatula (not a metal spoon as it will break up the rice) to cut the vinegar into the rice to ensure all corners of the rice have been mixed thoroughly in. It's best to use the rice while it's still warm, so it sticks together properly. Once it has completely cooled, it won't have the same sticky quality.

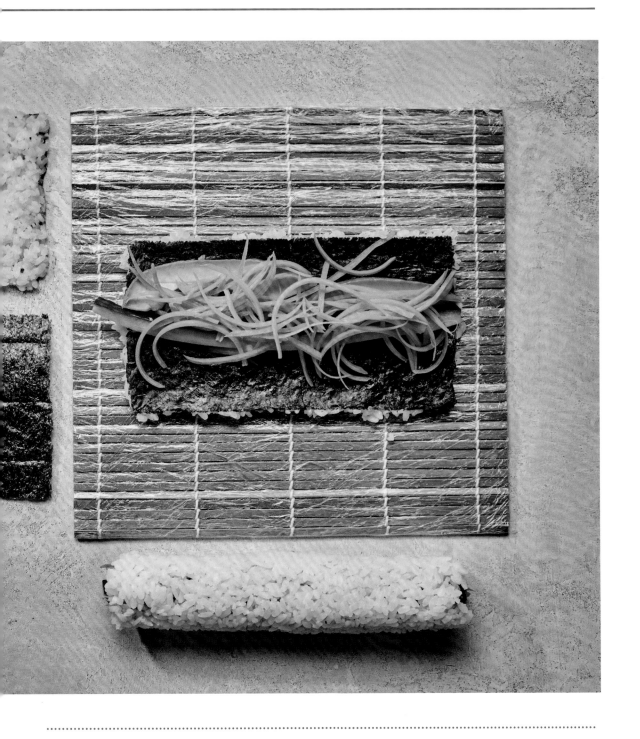

ROLLING MAKI

These rolls are the ones where the filling is rolled inside the seaweed. There are a couple of alternatives, below, too. To help shape the rolls, you'll need a bamboo rolling mat and clingfilm to cover it so that the nori stays dry and doesn't become soggy and tear.

For each maki, use around 90g (scant 3½oz/generous ⅓ cup) cooked sushi rice. These recipes call for 180g (6oz/scant 1 cup) dried weight of sushi rice which, once cooked, makes 360g (12½oz/generous 2 cups) cooked rice, so you'll have enough for 4 rolls or 20 nigiri. To stop the rice from sticking, have a bowl of water handy to wet your hands. Or if you prefer to wear gloves, oil them lightly with sunflower oil first. Here's the step-by-step guide below.

Step 1

Cover your rolling mat with clingfilm and put on a board. Place the nori sheet, shiny-side down, on the rolling mat. Gently spread the rice across the sheet leaving a 1cm (½in) border at the top and patting it out so that it's lying evenly to the edges of the other three sides.

Step 2

Add the filling, according to the recipe, so it sits horizontally along the long edge of the nori and about 1cm (½in) in from the bottom edge. Slide the nori down the mat, so it's in line with the edge of it.

Step 3

Use your fingers to hold the ingredients down and keep them secure. Tuck your thumbs underneath, then push the sushi mat forward in one swift movement up and over the filling, using your thumbs to help. Press the mat down to secure, then lift up the front and roll the mat further to finish rolling the maki. Make sure the seal is underneath, then press it again with the sushi mat. Remove the sushi mat and leave for around 1 minute for the edge of the nori to secure. Repeat this process for all four maki.

Step 4

Cut each in half with a sharp, fine-bladed knife, then each half into four pieces. If you find the knife sticks, run it under cold water but don't dry or lightly oil it.

URAMAKI

Once you've mastered a straightforward maki roll, making a uramaki – an inside-out roll – will seem like magic. The rice is spread all over the nori sheet, then the nori sheet is turned over so that the rice is on the outside. The moisture in the rice helps it stick to the nori, then it's pressed into shape with the sushi mat. When rolling up, leave a space between the edge of the mat and the nori (around 2.5cm/1in) to help make rolling easier.

FUTOMAKI

Where maki and uramaki make long thin rolls, a futomaki is a thick roll that is created by rolling up the nori from the shortest end.

NIGIRI

This is a small ball of cooked rice. Shape it into a small egg, then gently shape opposite ends into a slightly longer rectangular shape. Use your thumb and finger to gently press the sides and your other fingers to flatten the base. When covered, they should look long, round and curved. For these recipes, you'll need around 18g (scant ¾oz) cooked rice.

How to cut cucumber

Put the cucumber on a board and trim the ends. Slice lengthways in half. Slice one half in half lengthways again, then trim the seeds away with a knife.

Cut a quarter of the cucumber into long strips, 22cm (8½in) long and around 1cm (½in) thick. The cucumber needs to be thick enough so that when you eat it you can feel and taste the crunch of the cucumber. Trim away any excess seeds that might still be on the strip.

This piece will sit longer than the width of the nori, but it's trimmed off at the end. For a futomaki (shorter fat roll), cut the cucumber into 12–13cm (4½–5in) lengths.

How to cut salmon and tuna for nigiri and covering sushi rolls

For salmon, go to a fishmonger who sells sashimi-grade salmon – it must be super fresh and so will be safe to eat. Ask the fishmonger for a middle part of the fillet, around 25cm (10in) long and skinned and pin-boned, too. This will give you more than you need, but any excess can be used to make the long strips of salmon to fill a roll or chopped for toppings.

Put the salmon on a board and cut the thickest part of the salmon in the middle. To do this, lay the shortest end towards you and, starting at the top, follow the white spine in the middle, cut a couple of centimetres (just under an inch) in on either side. This will leave you with a thick, rectangular piece of salmon.

Cut the fillet into a block, the same length as a nori sheet. Starting at one end, angle the knife and slice on the diagonal (cutting on the bias of the fish) to cut the piece into thin slices, around 12g (scant ½oz) each. Each piece will measure around 0.5cm long, 2.5cm wide and 0.5cm thick (¼in long, 1in wide and ¼in thick).

The outside trimmings can be cut into long lengths, around 0.5cm (¼in) thick to go in the middle of the rolls. Or it can be finely chopped for a topping. Chill or freeze the outside bits if you're not going to use them immediately.

For tuna nigiri, again you need to buy sashimi-grade tuna. Ask the fishmonger for a piece from a tuna loin around 8cm (3¼in) long. Traditional sashimi chefs work with the whole loin but, for our recipes, you can adapt a much smaller piece. Essentially, you want to cut the loin down into a block, about 3cm (1¼in) high and 3cm (1¼in) wide and around 8cm (3¼in) long, so you have a piece that you can work with. Cut the top off first, so that you can get the height to around 3cm (1¼in) high. Then trim either side to make it 3cm (1¼in) wide. Slice pieces, along the width so that they're around 12g (scant ½oz) each. Use any leftovers, finely chopped, in other recipes or freeze for another time.

巻き寿司

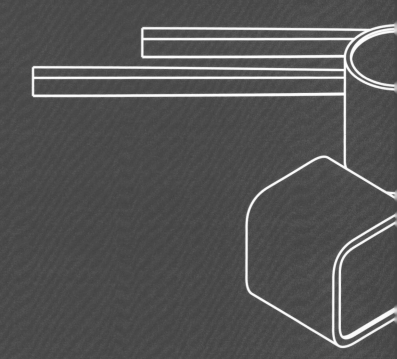

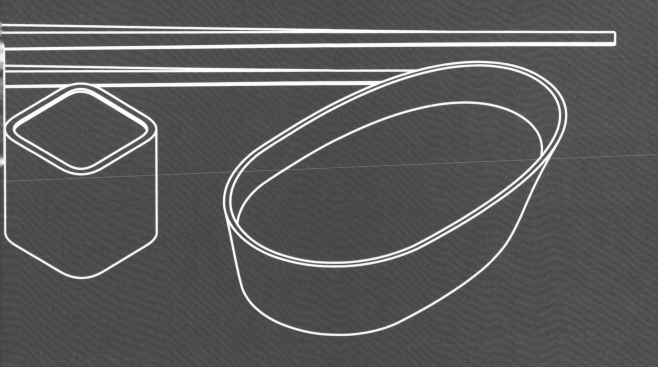

アボカド巻き　　　*AVOCADO MAKI*

❇ FOR AVOCADO MAKI

180g (6oz/scant 1 cup) sushi rice

3 tbsp seasoned vinegar for sushi rice

4 nori half sheets

½ firm ripe avocado, sliced
  lengthways into 8 slices

❇ TO SERVE

soy sauce, wasabi and sushi ginger

Here is another simple roll, filled with a slice of creamy avocado.

Make the rice according to the instructions on page 14 using 220ml (8floz/1 cup) water and the seasoned vinegar. Divide the rice roughly into four portions.

Place a sheet of nori on top of the sushi mat, shiny-side down and with the longest edge lying horizontally.

Spread out a portion of the rice on top, leaving a border of around 1cm (½in), then lay 2 slices of the avocado horizontally along the long edge, around a third of the way up.

Lift up the mat from the bottom over the avocado and press down. Continue to roll the sushi up and away from you, finishing with the seam lying underneath the roll. Press down to seal, remove the mat, and rest for 1 minute.

Set the first roll aside, then do the same again with the other three sheets of nori, and remaining rice and avocado. Slice each roll in half, then each half into four pieces.

Serve with the soy sauce, wasabi and sushi ginger.

かっぱ巻き　　CUCUMBER MAKI

❋ FOR CUCUMBER MAKI

180g (6oz/scant 1 cup) sushi rice
3 tbsp seasoned vinegar for sushi rice
4 nori half sheets
4 long sticks of cucumber

❋ TO SERVE

soy sauce, wasabi and sushi ginger

If this is your first time making sushi, here's a great recipe to start with. Both this and the avocado maki only contain one filling ingredient each, so are easy to roll up. They're also the most simple form of sushi – maki – where the sheet of nori seaweed lies on the outside.

Make the rice according to the instructions on page 14 using 220ml (8floz/1 cup) water and the seasoned vinegar. Divide the rice roughly into four portions.

Fill a small bowl with cold water.

Line the sushi mat with clingfilm and place a sheet of nori on top, shiny-side down and with the longest edge lying horizontally.

Spread out a portion of the rice, leaving a border at the top of around 1cm (½in). Lay a long stick of cucumber horizontally along the bottom edge, around a third in from the bottom.

Lift up the mat from the bottom over the cucumber and press down. Continue to roll the sushi up and away from you, finishing with the seam lying underneath the roll. Press down to seal so the seam is underneath, remove the mat and rest for 1 minute.

Set the first roll aside, then do the same again with the other three sheets of nori, and remaining rice and cucumber. Slice each roll in half, then each half into four pieces. Serve with the soy sauce, wasabi and sushi ginger.

カリカリ野菜巻き   *VEGGIE CRUNCH ROLLS*

180g (6oz/scant 1 cup) sushi rice

3 tbsp seasoned vinegar for sushi rice

4 nori half sheets

4 long slices of cucumber

1 small carrot, around 80g (3oz), cut
    into very fine matchsticks

8 slices avocado

teriyaki sauce, to drizzle

Spicy Mayo (see page 30), to drizzle

ready-made fried onions, to sprinkle

❋ TO SERVE

soy sauce, wasabi and sushi ginger

**The combination of crisp vegetables, sweet teriyaki sauce, spicy mayo
and crisp fried onions is sublime here.**

Make the rice according to the instructions on page 14, using 220ml (8fl oz/1 cup)
water and the seasoned vinegar. Divide the rice roughly into four portions.

Put a sheet of nori on top of the sushi mat, shiny-side down and with the longest
edge lying horizontally. Spread a portion of the rice to cover, then flip the nori
over. Arrange a length of cucumber in the middle of the nori, followed by the
carrot, spreading it out to the ends. Add a couple of slices of avocado and spread
out again so it is even. Roll up to make an inside-out roll. Do the same again to
make three more rolls.

Slice each into eight pieces, then drizzle with the teriyaki sauce, a little spicy mayo
and top with the fried onions. Serve with soy sauce, wasabi and sushi ginger.

山葵海老   *WASABI EBI*

Serves
4

6–8 pieces ready-made prawn
   tempura
180g (6oz/scant 1 cup) sushi rice
3 tbsp seasoned vinegar for sushi rice
4 thin asparagus spears, trimmed
4 nori half sheets
2 avocadoes, halved and stoned

❋ TO GARNISH

1–2 tbsp mayonnaise
   wasabi, to taste
1–2 tbsp ikura (red caviar) or other
   fish roe
soy sauce and sushi ginger, to serve

The bright green coat of this inside-out roll is made from finely sliced pieces of avocado, spread out like a deck of cards on top of the rice. Use a sharp knife to cut through the avocado easily.

Preheat the oven to 220°C/425°F/gas mark 7.

Put the prawns on a baking sheet and bake for 17–18 minutes until golden brown. Turn halfway through so they're golden all over. Cool and slice each in half lengthways.

Make the rice according to the instructions on page 14, using 220ml (8fl oz/1 cup) water and the seasoned vinegar. Divide the rice roughly into four portions.

Steam the asparagus in a pan of boiling water for 2–3 minutes until they turn bright green and are just tender. Lift out and cool under cold running water. Slice each in half lengthways.

Put a nori sheet onto the sushi mat, shiny-side down and with the longest edge lying horizontally. Spread a portion of sushi rice over the nori to cover. Turn the nori over so it is facing upwards.

Put 3–4 pieces of prawn tempura and a slice of asparagus in the middle of the sheet, lying horizontally across. Roll up to make an inside-out-roll. Do the same again to make three more rolls.

Carefully peel the avocado halves. Lay one horizontally on a board. Carefully slice the avocado at a 45° angle into very thin slices, around 1mm (⅛in) thick. Lift up with a knife and spread out on to one of the rolls so that the avocado covers all the rice. Cover with a sheet of clingfilm and lay the sushi mat on top. Press your hands all the way along to reshape the roll to help the avocado stick to the rice. Do the same with the other rolls.

To garnish, mix the mayonnaise and a touch of wasabi together in a bowl. Taste to check the balance is right.

Slice each roll into eight pieces, then put a small blob of wasabi mayo on top of each. Decorate the mayo with the ikura and serve with the soy sauce and sushi ginger.

サーモンタルタル

CRUNCHY RICE SALMON TARTARE

400g (14oz/2 cups) sushi rice

6 tbsp seasoned vinegar for sushi rice

sunflower or vegetable oil, for frying

200g (7oz) fresh sashimi-grade
    salmon (see page 17), finely chopped

10g (¼oz) sushi ginger, finely
    chopped

1 tsp soy sauce

1 tsp mirin

❊ TO GARNISH

black and white sesame seeds

edible flowers and/or coriander micro
    herbs, optional

❊ TO SERVE

soy sauce, wasabi and sushi ginger

For this recipe, the sushi rice is cooked as in other recipes, then rolled into a thick log. The crunchy element comes from a short spell of deep-frying, so each piece becomes a little cup to hold a portion of perfectly seasoned fresh salmon. It's one of our absolute favourites!

Make the rice according to the instructions on page 14, using 480ml (17fl oz/generous 2 cups) water and the seasoned vinegar. Holding the pan with one hand to steady it, use the other hand to squeeze the rice as much as you can to meld it together. Continue to do this until all the rice is sticking together easily and it looks quite smooth.

Roughly split the rice into two and lift one portion onto the middle of a sushi mat, spreading it out along the width. Wrap the mat around it and begin to shape it into a log. It will be much bigger than making other sushi as it's double the quantity of rice. Keep rolling and shaping, pulling the mat tighter on the rice, until it's set in an even log.

Do the same with the other portion of rice and transfer both pieces to the freezer for 3 minutes to set.

Meanwhile, heat the oil in a large saucepan or deep-fat fryer to 190°C/375°F or until a breadcrumb sizzles when dropped into the oil. Line a plate with kitchen paper.

Carefully lower a log into the hot oil and cook until golden, about 3–4 minutes. If your pan isn't big enough, cut each log in half to make two shorter logs. Lift out and drain on the kitchen paper and continue to cook all the pieces. Transfer to the freezer to chill for 4 minutes.

Lift onto a board. Wet a very sharp knife and use to trim the ends from each log. The point of the knife needs to be pointed down around the roll so that the main part of the knife comes down quickly and evenly through the crispy rice. If you've cooked the logs whole, cut each into around 12 slices. The smaller logs will cut into around 6 slices. Lay the pieces flat on a platter.

Mix the salmon, ginger, soy sauce and mirin together in a separate bowl. Use a teaspoon to spoon a small portion onto each piece, then garnish with the sesame seeds, edible flowers and/or micro herbs, if desired.

鉄火巻き　　　　*TUNA CRUNCH ROLLS*

❋ FOR MAKI

4 pieces ready-made prawn tempura
180g (6oz/scant 1 cup) sushi rice
3 tbsp seasoned rice for sushi rice
100g (3½oz) sashimi-grade tuna
　(see page 17), finely chopped
¼–½ tsp Spicy Mayo (see page 30)
4 nori half sheets
4 strips of cucumber, around
　12–13cm (4½–5in) long

❋ TO GARNISH

1–2 tsp eel sauce, optional
2 spring onions, finely sliced
ready-made fried onions,
　to sprinkle
sesame seeds, to sprinkle

These big fat rolls come courtesy of the futomaki method of rolling sushi. Instead of laying the nori sheet horizontally on the sushi mat, it's put down lengthways, so you roll up from the short end to make a much bigger roll. The sliced sushi, filled with tempura prawns and cucumber, are then laid down flat and topped with a combination of fresh tuna, spicy mayo and – for the crunch – crispy fried onions. There's a drizzle of eel sauce on there, too, which is a thick Japanese sauce made from soy, mirin and sugar (and no eel!), delivering a touch of sweetness at the end.

Preheat the oven to 220°C/425°F/gas mark 7.

Put the prawns on a baking sheet and bake for 17–18 minutes until golden brown. Turn halfway through so they're golden all over. Cool and slice each in half lengthways.

Make the rice according to the instructions on page 14, using 220ml (8fl oz/1 cup) water and the seasoned vinegar. Divide the rice roughly into four portions.

While the rice is cooking, mix the tuna in a bowl with the spicy mayo – it will act as a glue, helping the tuna pieces to stick together and is also essential for spooning it onto the rounds of sushi.

Put a nori sheet, shiny-side down, on the sushi mat, with the shortest end towards you. Spread a portion of the sushi rice on the nori, leaving about 2cm (¾in) border at the top. Put one strip of cucumber and 2 pieces of prawn tempura in the middle. Use the mat to roll into a thick sushi roll or futomaki. Do the same with the remaining ingredients to make 3 more rolls.

Cut each roll into six pieces. Lay them down on a platter. Spoon a small amount of spicy tuna onto each piece.

Top with a drizzle of eel sauce, if using, spring onion, some crispy onions and sesame seeds.

カリカリサーモン巻き *SALMON CRUNCH ROLLS*

❋ FOR MAKI

180g (6oz/scant 1 cup) sushi rice

3 tbsp seasoned vinegar for sushi

4 nori half sheets

4 long sticks of cucumber

around 75g (3oz) sashimi-grade
 salmon (see page 17), sliced into
 4 long strips

8 slices of avocado

teriyaki sauce, to drizzle

Spicy Mayo (see page 30), to drizzle

ready-made fried onions, to sprinkle

❋ TO SERVE

soy sauce, wasabi and sushi ginger

Here's our classic California roll – cucumber, avocado and salmon – wrapped in an inside-out roll, then finished with a drizzle of teriyaki sauce and spicy mayo, plus a sprinkling of moreish crispy onions.

Make the rice according to the instructions on page 14, using 220ml (8fl oz/1 cup) water and the seasoned vinegar. Divide the rice roughly into four portions.

Place a nori sheet on the sushi mat, shiny side down and with the longest edge lying horizontally. Spread a portion of rice all over the nori, then turn the nori over so it is facing upwards.

Put a stick of cucumber in the middle, then add a strip of salmon. Tuck a couple of slices of avocado on top. Roll up to make an inside-out roll (see page 16). Do the same again to make three more rolls.

Slice each roll into eight. With the 8 pieces still in a roll shape, drizzle over the teriyaki sauce and then the mayo. Scatter over the fried onions to cover the top.

Serve with the soy sauce, wasabi and sushi ginger.

特上サーモン巻き　　*SALMON TEMPTATION*

Serves
4

❊ FOR THE AVOCADO AND CUCUMBER INSIDE-OUT ROLL

180g (6oz/scant 1 cup) sushi rice

3 tbsp seasoned vinegar for sushi rice

4 nori half sheets

1–2 tsp aonori seaweed

4 long pieces of cucumber

8 slices of avocado

around 50g (2oz) sashimi-grade salmon (see page 17), finely chopped

small handful chives, finely chopped, to garnish

12g (scant ½oz) shichimi powder

❊ FOR THE SPICY MAYO

3 tbsp mayonnaise

1 tsp Sriracha chilli sauce

1 tsp shichimi powder

❊ TO SERVE

soy sauce, wasabi and sushi ginger

A simple avocado and cucumber inside-out roll, rolled in aonori seaweed (flaked seaweed) for texture and flavour, is crowned with a spoonful of chopped fresh salmon. It's both eye-catching and delicious.

Make the rice according to the instructions on page 14, using 220ml (8fl oz/1 cup) water and the seasoned vinegar. Divide the rice roughly into four portions.

Make the spicy mayo by mixing together the mayonnaise, Sriracha chilli sauce and the shichimi powder in a small bowl. Set aside.

Put a nori sheet on top of the sushi mat, shiny-side down and with the longest edge lying horizontally. Spread a portion of the sushi rice all over the nori to cover, then sprinkle over a little of the aonori. Flip the nori over so the shiny side is uppermost. Place 1 piece of cucumber and 2 slices of avocado in the middle and roll up. Do the same to make three more rolls.

Slice each roll into eight pieces and arrange on a plate so they each sit on their edges.

Spoon a little spicy mayo on top of each piece, then top each with the finely chopped salmon.

Sprinkle a few chives over each one, followed by a little shichimi powder. Serve with the soy sauce, wasabi and sushi ginger.

サーモン巻き　　*DOUBLE SALMON ROLL*

❋ FOR THE INSIDE-OUT MAKI

180g (6oz/scant 1 cup) sushi rice

3 tbsp seasoned vinegar for sushi rice

4 nori half sheets

4 thin strips of sashmi-grade salmon
(see page 17), each around 21cm
(around 8¼in) long and 0.5cm (¼in)
thick

4 long slices of cucumber

8–12 slices avocado

❋ TO COVER

1 avocado, halved and stoned

around 20 thin slices of sashimi-grade
salmon

❋ TO SERVE

soy sauce, wasabi and sushi
ginger

With fresh salmon on the inside and layers on the outside, too these are rather clever as half the rolls are covered in salmon and half are covered in avocado slices. When you cut them into pieces, each roll is put back together, this time alternating the salmon roll and the avocado roll.

Make the rice according to the instructions on page 14, using 220ml (8fl oz/1 cup) water and the seasoned vinegar. Divide the rice roughly into four portions.

First make an inside-out maki. Place a nori sheet on the sushi mat, shiny-side down with the longest edge lying horizontally. Spread a portion of the sushi rice across the nori to cover completely. Turn the nori over so the nori faces upwards.

Lay a strip of salmon lengthways in the middle of the nori, then do the same with the cucumber and 2–3 slices of avocado, ensuring the avocado is evenly spread.

Holding the ingredients securely in the middle with your fingers of both hands, roll the mat over and press so that half the roll is set. Then lift up the mat and roll it forward again so that the sushi is completely rolled, with the seam underneath. Remove the mat. Do the same to make 3 more rolls.

Peel the avocado and lay one half on a board. Finely slice at a 45° angle, into 1mm (less than ⅛in) slices. Use a long, sharp knife to lift the avocado up and onto the roll and spread out gently to cover the rice. Cover a second roll in this way. Cover each with clingfilm and press the mat on top, shaping to help the avocado stick to the rice.

Wrap around 10 slices of salmon over the top of each of the remaining rolls, spreading them out evenly, so that both are covered in salmon.

Slice each roll into eight pieces, then alternate each of the salmon rolls with each of the avocado rolls.

Arrange on plates and serve with soy sauce, wasabi and sushi ginger.

鮭とマグロの握り　SALMON AND TUNA SUSHI

❋ FOR THE RICE

180g (6oz/scant 1 cup) sushi rice

3 tbsp seasoned vinegar for sushi rice

❋ FOR THE SALMON NIGIRI

10 slices sashimi-grade salmon (see
page 17)

❋ FOR THE TUNA NIGIRI

10 slices sashimi-grade tuna (see
page 17)

❋ TO SERVE

soy sauce, wasabi and sushi ginger

Here's another simple recipe. The rice is shaped into little ovals, then topped with slices of very fresh fish. A sharp fish knife is key here to slice the fish into super-thin layers that lie smoothly on top of the rice. If you like, dab a little wasabi on top of the rice before laying a slice of fish on top.

Make the rice according to the instructions on page 14, using 220ml (8fl oz/1 cup) water and the seasoned vinegar. Divide the rice roughly into four portions.

Divide each portion again into five portions, then shape each one into an oval. Place on a plate while you shape the rest of the rice to make around 20 pieces in total.

Lay a piece of salmon onto half the rice shapes, then the tuna onto the other half.

Serve with all the accompaniments.

イカのカラマリ巻き　*LUXURY CALAMARI ROLLS*

4–6 pieces ready-made prawn
　tempura
180g (6oz/scant 1 cup) sushi rice
3 tbsp seasoned vinegar for sushi rice
4 nori half sheets
4 long pieces of cucumber
8 slices of avocado
2–4 tsp Spicy Mayo (see page 30),
　depending on how spicy you like it
2 spring onions, finely sliced

❋ FOR THE CALAMARI SALAD

300g (10½oz) squid tubes, cut into
　rings
2–3g (just under ⅛oz) dried black
　fungus mushrooms, soaked in a
　bowl of warm water for 30 minutes,
　drained and very finely chopped
20g (¾oz) bamboo shoots, finely
　chopped
10g (¼oz) sushi ginger, finely
　chopped
a good pinch of caster sugar
2 tbsp seasoned vinegar for sushi rice
1–2 tsp sesame oil
sea salt

❋ TO SERVE

soy sauce, wasabi and sushi ginger

These double fish rolls are a treat. The maki sushi is filled with avocado, cucumber and prawn tempura, then topped with a pickled calamari salad. If you can make the salad a day ahead, even better – the squid will be even more flavoursome as it will have had more time to pickle.

Preheat the oven to 220°C/425°F/gas mark 7. Spread the prawns out on a baking sheet and bake for 17–18 minutes until golden. Turn halfway through so that they bake evenly. Set aside to cool. Slice each in half lengthways.

Make the calamari salad. Bring a small pan of boiling water to the boil and cook the squid for 3–4 minutes until the rings have turned white and feel tender when pierced with a fork or sharp knife. Drain well and cool quickly by spreading out on a plate.

Once cool, chop the squid into small pieces and put in a bowl. Add the mushrooms, bamboo shoots, sushi ginger, sugar, vinegar and sesame oil. Season with salt and set aside.

Make the rice according to the instructions on page 14, using 220ml (8fl oz/1 cup) water and the seasoned vinegar. Divide the rice roughly into four portions.

Place a nori sheet onto a sushi mat, shiny-side down and the longest edge lying horizontally. Spread a portion of the sushi rice over the nori, leaving a 1cm (½in) border at the top. Place a piece of cucumber in the middle of the rice, followed by a couple of avocado slices. Top with 2–3 pieces of the prawn tempura. Roll up and set aside, then make the other three maki rolls.

Slice each roll into eight pieces, then turn each piece on its side to sit flat. Top each with a little spicy mayo. Spoon some calamari salad onto each, garnish with the spring onions and serve with the soy sauce, wasabi and sushi ginger.

スパイシー エビ天巻き

SPICY PRAWN TEMPURA ROLLS

Serves
4

4–8 pieces ready-made prawn
tempura, depending on the
thickness of each piece
180g (6oz/scant 1 cup) sushi rice
3 tbsp seasoned vinegar for sushi rice
4 nori half sheets
2 tsp each black and white sesame
seeds
½ firm ripe avocado, sliced
lengthways into 8 slices
4 long sticks of cucumber

❋ TO SERVE
Spicy Mayo (see page 30)
soy sauce, wasabi and sushi ginger

See photograph overleaf.

Here are elements of a prawn cocktail, wrapped up in an inside-out roll. The difference is that it's served with a spicy mayo to give a mouth-tingling chilli flavour.

Preheat the oven to 220°C/425°F/gas mark 7.

Put the prawn tempura on a baking sheet and bake for 17–18 minutes until golden brown. Turn halfway through so they're golden all over. Once cooked and cooled, halve the prawns lengthways.

Make the rice according to the instructions on page 14, using 220ml (8fl oz/1 cup) water and the seasoned vinegar. Divide the rice roughly into four portions.

Put a nori sheet on the sushi mat, shiny-side down, with the longest edge lying horizontally. Spread a portion of the sushi rice all over the nori to cover it evenly. Sprinkle over the mixed sesame seeds. Turn the nori sheet over, so the rice is facing downwards.

Put 2 slices of avocado, a piece of cucumber and 1–2 pieces of the prawn tempura in the middle of the nori.

Keeping the edge of the nori sheet close to the edge of the mat, hold the ingredients with the four fingers of each hand, then use your thumbs to start rolling the mat and flip it over the ingredients. Press down firmly, then lift the mat up and continue to roll it forwards so that the sushi is rolled up. Press down firmly again using the mat. Remove the mat and rest for 1 minute.

Repeat to make three more rolls.

Trim the sides of each roll – you can leave one end with a prawn tail peeking out if you like – then slice each roll into eight pieces. Serve with the spicy mayo and the usual accompaniments.

サーモンの生春巻き　*CRISTAL SALMON ROLLS*

Serves
4

120g (4½oz/¾ cup) sushi rice

2 tbsp seasoned vinegar for sushi rice

4 x 22cm (9in) Vietnamese rice paper
 rounds

around 50g (2oz) lettuce leaves, such
 as iceberg

around 4 tbsp cream cheese

8 slices avocado

8 long slices of cucumber

120g (4½oz) sashimi-grade salmon
 (see page 17), cut into 4 long strips

around 40g (1½oz) tobiko fish roe

around 12 mint leaves

around 8 coriander sprigs

❋ TO SERVE

soy sauce, wasabi and sushi ginger

These refreshing rolls combine a rice-paper wrap with crisp lettuce, fresh salmon, a slick of cream cheese and a luxurious smattering of ruby-red tobiko fish roe.

Make the rice following the instructions on page 14, using 145ml (5fl oz/generous ½ cup) water and the seasoned vinegar. Divide roughly into four portions.

Make a cristal roll. Fill a large bowl with warm water and soak a rice round in it for around 20 seconds (see page 76). It's ready when it feels slightly floppy and silky when you pull it out of the water and the time will depend on the temperature of the water. Make sure that it doesn't soften so much that it breaks up – it will soften more out of the water. Drain and place on a chopping board.

Add some lettuce leaves to cover the rice paper, leaving about a 1cm (½in) border around the edge. Flatten the lettuce down so that it sticks to the paper.

Spread a portion of the sushi rice in a thin layer over the top. Spread a quarter of the cream cheese thinly over the top of the rice and top with a quarter each of the avocado, cucumber and salmon. Sprinkle over a quarter of the tobiko and herbs, then roll up tightly, tucking the rice paper in at the sides. Repeat with the remaining ingredients to make three more rolls.

Leave each to set for about 1 minute, then cut the rolls in half, then cut each half into three, to make six pieces for each person.

Serve with the soy sauce, wasabi and sushi ginger.

豆腐の握り   *TOFU NIGIRI*

Serves
4

180g (6oz/scant 1 cup) sushi rice

3 tbsp seasoned vinegar for sushi rice

around 275g (9½oz/1½ cups) firm
   tofu, drained and pressed (see tip
   on page 70)

wasabi, to taste, optional

2 nori half sheets, each cut into
   10 strips lengthways

❋ TO SERVE
soy sauce and sushi ginger

**Here's a vegetarian alternative to tuna and salmon nigiri. You cook the
rice in exactly the same way, then slice pieces of pressed tofu and secure
on top of the rice with a strip of nori seaweed. Sneak a dab of wasabi
onto the rice before putting the tofu on top for a little kick of heat.**

Make the rice according to the instructions on page 14, using 220ml (8floz/
1 cup) water and the seasoned vinegar.

Use a tablespoon measure to measure out 20 portions of sushi rice, each weighing
18g (just under ¾oz). Roll each piece into an oval shape and tap the bottom so
that it sits flat.

Cut the tofu into 20 slices, each measuring around 3 x 8cm (1¼ x 3¼in) and 3mm
(about ⅛in) thick. Use the end of a chopstick or tip of a knife to put a dab of
wasabi onto the top of the rice, if desired.

Lay a piece of tofu on top of each portion of rice, then wrap a nori strip around
both to secure, snipping the end off if necessary. The moisture from the rice will
seal the end. Serve with the soy sauce and sushi ginger.

See photograph on page 43.

野菜寿司セット　*GREEN TEMPTATION*

✽ FOR THE QUINOA AND AVOCADO ROLLS – MAKES 4

45g (1¾oz/¼ cup) red quinoa, soaked in a bowl of cold water for 30 minutes

135g (5oz/⅔ cup) sushi rice

3 tbsp seasoned vinegar for sushi rice

4 nori half sheets

8 slices of avocado

✽ FOR THE VEGGIE CALIFORNIA ROLLS WITH CHIVES – MAKES 2

180g (6oz/scant 1 cup) sushi rice

3 tbsp seasoned vinegar for sushi rice

2 nori half sheets

aonori seaweed, for sprinkling

2 long slices of cucumber

4–6 avocado slices

16g (just over ½oz) whole chives

✽ TO SERVE

soy sauce, wasabi and sushi ginger

Different types of sushi come together in this vegetarian feast with a couple of twists. Red quinoa combined with the sushi rice gives the maki rolls a slightly nutty texture. In contrast, a handful of chives elevates the classic vegetarian Cali inside-out roll. We also like adding Tofu Nigiri (see page 41 and photographed here) to this green feast.

Drain the quinoa and put in a pan with the sushi rice for those rolls (see intro for tips). Cook following the instructions on page 14, using 220ml (8fl oz/1 cup) water.

Cook the sushi rice for the Cali rollls in a separate pan following the instructions on page 14 using 220ml (8fl oz/1 cup) water. Add the vinegar to each and stir in.

Make the quinoa and avocado rolls. Put a nori sheet onto the sushi mat, shiny-side down and with the longest edge lying horizontally along the mat. Spread a portion of the sushi rice over the nori, leaving a 1cm (½in) border at the top. Put 2 slices of avocado in the middle, lengthways, and roll up. Continue to make three more rolls. Cut each roll into eight pieces.

For the veggie Cali rolls, make an inside-out roll, following the instructions on page 44 for the recipe for the Secret Garden Rolls.

Arrange the pieces on platters and serve with soy sauce, wasabi and sushi ginger.

謎の野菜巻き　　*SECRET GARDEN ROLLS*

180g (6oz/scant 1 cup) sushi rice

3 tbsp seasoned vinegar for sushi rice

1–2 tsp aonori seaweed, for
  sprinkling

4 long pieces of cucumber

8 avocado slices

16g (just over ½oz) whole chives

❁ **TO SERVE**

soy sauce, wasabi and sushi ginger

There's a lovely contrast here in this uramaki roll between the cool refreshing cucumber, creamy avocado and subtle onion tang from the chives. The whole roll is finished with aonori (flaked seaweed).

Make the rice according to the instructions on page 14, using 220ml (8fl oz/1 cup) water and the seasoned vinegar. Divide the rice roughly into four portions.

Put a sheet of the nori onto a sushi mat, shiny-side down and with the longest edge lying horizontally. Spread a portion of the sushi rice all over the nori to cover, then sprinkle a little of the aonori on top. Flip the nori over, then put a piece of cucumber, a couple of slices of avocado and a quarter of the chives in the middle. You may need to separate out the chives so that they sit evenly along the length of the nori sheet. Roll up using the sushi mat to help.

Do the same again with the rest of the ingredients to make four rolls. Cut each into eight pieces and serve with the soy sauce, wasabi and sushi ginger.

スパイシーエビと マンゴー巻き

MANGO TANGO ROLLS

Serves
4

6–8 pieces ready-made prawn
  tempura
180g (6oz/scant 1 cup) sushi rice
3 tbsp seasoned vinegar for sushi rice
4 nori half sheets
12g (scant ½oz) whole chives
2 medium firm-but-ripe mangoes

❁ TO GARNISH
Spicy Mayo (see page 30) and
shichimi powder

❁ TO SERVE
soy sauce, wasabi and sushi ginger

You need just-ripe mangoes for this recipe – too hard and there won't be the sweetness to marry with the prawns and spicy mayo. Too soft and the mangoes will be difficult to slice and shape on the roll.

Preheat the oven to 220°C/425°F/gas mark 7.

Put the prawns on a baking sheet and bake for 17–18 minutes until golden brown. Turn halfway through so they're golden all over. Cool and slice each in half lengthways.

Make the rice according to the instructions on page 14, using 220ml (8fl oz/1 cup) water and the seasoned vinegar. Divide the rice roughly into four portions.

Put a nori sheet onto a sushi mat, shiny-side down and with the longest edge lying horizontally. Spread a portion of the sushi rice all over to cover. Turn the nori over so it is facing upwards. Put 3–4 prawn halves and a quarter of the chives in the middle, separating the chives out so they spread to the sides. Roll up to make an inside-out roll. Do the same again to make three more rolls.

Put each mango on a board and, using a thin-bladed, sharp knife, slice either side of the stone. Peel each half. Lay one half on the board and slice horizontally to create very thin ovals. Keep it in its shape while you do the other 3 pieces.

Put the mango slices from one half on top of one of the rolls and spread out like a pack of cards (this is the same technique as the avocado in the Wasabi Ebi roll, see page 24). Cover with clingfilm and press and shape again into a round with a rolling mat. Cut into eight pieces. Put a dot of spicy mayo on top of each piece, then sprinkle over a little shichimi powder. Do the same with the other three rolls and mango slices and serve with the soy sauce, wasabi and sushi ginger.

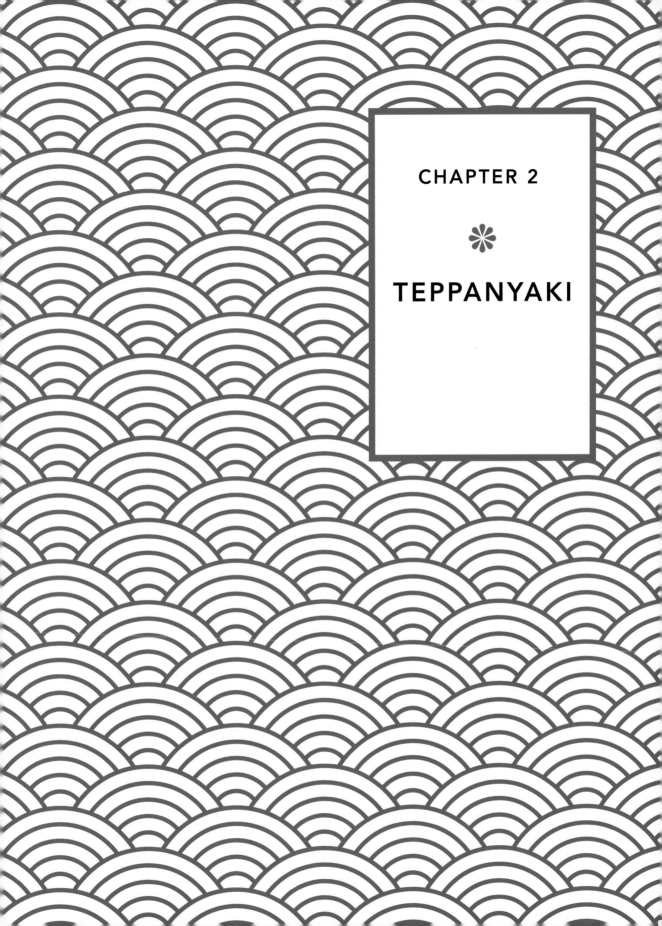

CHAPTER 2

*

TEPPANYAKI

食いしん坊

kuishinbou

—

A person who loves to eat like crazy.

If you've ever been to a teppanyaki restaurant, there's a theatrical element to the way the food is cooked and presented. The huge teppan grill – a large rectangular hot plate that often sits flush to the work surface – will be headed up by a chef cooking the food in the seated area of the restaurant, rather than out of sight in a separate kitchen. It's a demo-style delight with seats all around the chef where you can watch your selection of raw ingredients cooked to perfection right in front of you.

With the temperature of the hot plate soaring, this is where the magic happens. As marinated fresh meat, fish or vegetables, slick with oil, are added to the teppan, you can watch whatever you've chosen be cooked to perfection, right before your very eyes. The whole experience is a feast for all the senses as you watch the chef in action, hear the ingredients sizzling, smell the wonderful aromas rising from the hot plate, and your mouth will be watering as the cooked dish is presented to you.

This is super-fast cooking at its very best, so in order to achieve these same results at home, follow a few simple rules. Use a heavy-based pan that can withstand high temperatures and have a neutral oil – such as a sunflower or vegetable oil – that has a high smoking point to hand. Measure and prepare all your ingredients first and have them ready in small dishes or ramekins so that you're ready to go with the dressing as soon as the main bits and pieces are cooked.

There is something for every day of the week in this chapter. The Stir-fried Rice with Vegetables (see page 66) is great for those nights when time is short. If the rice is already cooked, this becomes an almost instant supper when teamed with a large handful of vegetables, all chopped into similar-sized chunks so they cook evenly. Throw in a couple of eggs and this transforms into the Classic Stir-fried Rice (see page 65), which is uber-nourishing, too. For a fancy supper, try Teppanyaki Duck (see page 54) – the rich sauce is cut through with a squeeze of orange for a touch of acidity, or the terrific Seafood Teppanyaki feast (see page 52) garnished with crumbled nori.

If you fancy something with noodles, there's plenty here. The Chicken Katsu Noodles (see page 68) is a bestseller for us, combining contrasting slices of crispy chicken with silken noodles dressed in a miso sauce. We're sure it will be as popular with you at home.

海鮮鉄板焼き丼　　*SEAFOOD TEPPANYAKI*

300g (10½oz/1½ cups) sushi rice

3 tbsp seasoned vinegar for sushi rice

150g (5oz) white fish (haddock, cod and pollock are all good), skinned and cubed

150g (5oz) salmon, skinned and cubed

1 large squid, cleaned and sliced

12 shelled scallops, without roe

12 mussels in shell, cleaned

1 tbsp sunflower or vegetable oil, plus a little extra

4–6 shiitake mushrooms, halved

4 spring onions, chopped

salt and freshly ground black pepper

❋ FOR THE DIPPING SAUCE
(OR SEE INTRO)

2 tbsp soy sauce

1 tbsp sake

1 tbsp mirin

a dash of sesame oil

2 thin slices of ginger

❋ TO SERVE

crumbled nori – you'll need around one half sheet

This feast is easy to prepare whether you're a seasoned fish cook or a novice. Everything's prepared so it's more or less the same size and cooks in the same time so all the pieces stay juicy. Aromatic rice is a must to soak up all the juices – use either sushi rice or the slightly lighter Jasmine rice, if you prefer. Instead of making the dipping sauce here, you could try Japanese sesame sauce, Ponzu sauce or Yum Yum sauce.

Put all the dipping sauce ingredients into a bowl. Whisk together and set aside.

Pour the rice into a sieve and rinse well. Put in a pan with 500ml (18fl oz/generous 2 cups) water and a good pinch of salt. Cover and bring to the boil. Turn down to the lowest setting and cook for 10 minutes, without lifting the lid. Take the pan off the heat, keeping the lid on, and set to one side while you cook the fish. As soon as the rice is cooked, drizzle over the seasoned vinegar and stir in. Keep the pan covered.

Heat a teppan or a large, flat frying pan until hot.

Put the white fish, salmon, squid, scallops and mussels into a large bowl. Drizzle the oil over the top, season, toss together and set aside.

Toss the shiitake mushrooms and spring onions in a little oil and season, then cook on the teppan or frying pan for 2–3 minutes until just golden and cooked through. Spoon into a bowl.

Add the white fish, salmon, squid and scallops to the pan and cook, in small batches if necessary, for 4–5 minutes each side, turning only once. Scoop out of the pan and set aside. Add the mussels to the pan and cook until they open. You may need to cover them with a lid at this stage to help them open. Pick out the mussel meat and discard the shells, then pop the mussel meat back into the pan – there should be some juices from cooking the mussels, too. Add the cooked seafood, fish, mushrooms and spring onions back into the pan and toss everything together to warm through.

Use a wooden spatula to spoon the rice onto a serving platter. Arrange the fish on top with the mushrooms and spring onions. Garnish with the nori seaweed and serve with the dipping sauce(s).

鴨の鉄板焼き　　*TEPPANYAKI DUCK*

Serves
4–6

4 duck breasts (around 675g/1½lb)
   total weight)
200ml (7fl oz/scant 1 cup) dry sake
4 tbsp light brown soft sugar
3 tbsp tamari soy sauce
5 tbsp freshly squeezed orange juice
   – around 1 large orange
4 spring onions, thinly sliced
freshly ground black pepper

Here's a match for the classic French dish *duck a l'orange*, but made in super-quick time on the teppan (or frying pan). It's important to render the fat by cooking the duck skin-side down first, so that the skin colours until golden and becomes crisp. If you can't get hold of sake, dry sherry or shaoxing wine makes a good swap here.

Put the duck breasts on a board and use a sharp knife to score the fat in a criss-cross pattern, taking care not to cut too deeply into the meat.

Place the duck breasts, skin-side down, into a large, heavy-based frying pan (or on the teppan) and start to heat it. Place the pan over a low-medium heat and cook until the fat begins to render.

Turn the heat up a notch and sauté the breasts until the skin is golden brown. Turn over and cook briefly for around 1–2 minutes.

Remove the duck breasts from the pan and set them aside. Drain the duck fat into a jar for another use.

Place the pan back onto the heat and add the sake and sugar. Bring to the boil to dissolve the sugar and cook off the alcohol. Simmer until the sake reduces by around a third. Add the soy sauce and orange juice, season with black pepper and stir together, simmering for around 1 minute more to cook everything together. Taste the sauce and if it seems too strong, add a splash of water. If it lacks flavour and tastes weak, add a splash of tamari.

Add the duck back to the pan, skin-side up, and simmer while basting the skin until the duck breasts are cooked to your liking – they're best served rosy pink.

Remove the pan from the heat and lift the duck onto a board. Add half the spring onions to the sauce and stir in. Slice the duck into thin slices.

Pour the sauce onto a platter, then arrange the duck on top and garnish with the remaining spring onions. Serve straightaway, on a bed of soba noodles, if you like.

牛肉の鉄板焼き　　BEEF TEPPANYAKI

400g (14oz) beef sirloin, cut across
the grain into 0.5cm (¼in) slices
1–2 tbsp sunflower or vegetable oil

❈ **FOR THE MARINADE**
3 tbsp soy sauce
2 tbsp sweet sherry, plus extra for
cooking
1 tbsp garlic powder
¼ tsp caster sugar
1 tsp freshly ground black pepper

This dish combines the simplicity of the teppan method with some classic Asian flavours and we've found that it is very moreish! A good quantity of ground black pepper gives this a subtle kick of heat, too.

Mix all the marinade ingredients together in a large bowl. Add the slices of beef and mix well. Leave to marinate for at least 1 hour. If you need to marinate the beef for any longer, put it in a sealable container and chill. Take it out of the fridge about 30 minutes before you want to cook it.

Heat a teppan or a large, flat frying pan until hot. Add the sunflower or vegetable oil and, as soon as the oil has heated and is covering the bottom of the pan, add the sliced beef (reserve the marinade) and fry for 2–3 minutes until golden on each side. It should still be a little pink in the middle. Place on a warm serving dish.

Reduce the heat to low and, using the same teppan or pan, add the leftover marinade plus 1 tablespoon more of the sherry. Simmer for 1–2 minutes or until the sauce has thickened a little.

Pour the sauce on top of the beef and serve straightaway.

SPRING ROLLS

50g (2oz) vermicelli rice noodles,
    broken into small pieces

1 tbsp sesame oil

½ Chinese cabbage, very finely sliced

large handful of beansprouts

½ large carrot, cut into sticks

2 garlic cloves, finely chopped

2cm (¾in) piece fresh root ginger,
    finely chopped

1 tbsp soy sauce

1 tbsp shaoxing rice wine

2 spring onions, finely sliced

1 tbsp freshly chopped coriander

1 tbsp cornflour

1 packet spring roll sheets, 15cm
    (6in) diameter

salt

sunflower or vegetable oil, for frying

✽ TO STORE

Keep the spring rolls for up to three
days in the fridge. If you want to
freeze them, open-freeze on a baking
sheet until firm, then pack into an
airtight container, layered with baking
parchment and freeze for up to one
month.

✽ TO COOK FROM CHILLED

Preheat the oven to 200°C/400°F/gas
mark 6. Brush the rolls with a little
sunflower or vegetable oil. Put on a
baking sheet and cook for 20 minutes
until pale golden.

✽ TO COOK FROM FROZEN

As above, but cook for 30 minutes
until golden.

**This recipe makes around 30 rolls, but you only need around 8 for the
noodle bowl dish. Store the wrappers and filling in the fridge if you only
want to make that amount and then wrap and finish the others within a
day, when you have more time.**

Soak the noodles in a bowl of warm water for 8–10 minutes until softened. Drain.

Heat the sesame oil in a wok or heavy-based pan over a medium-high heat. Add
the cabbage, beansprouts and carrot and stir-fry for 3–4 minutes, stirring until
starting to soften.

Add the garlic and ginger and cook for 2 more minutes, then add the soy sauce,
rice wine, spring onions and coriander.

Transfer to a bowl, then stir in the noodles and leave to cool. Drain off any excess
juices at the bottom of the bowl as they'll make the spring rolls soggy.

Put the cornflour into a small bowl and stir in 3 tablespoons water – this is to help
stick down and secure the edges of the spring roll wrappers.

Next, fill the spring rolls. Lay a sheet of spring roll pastry on a board, with one
corner facing towards you.

Place about 1 tablespoon of the vegetable mixture around a third up from the
bottom of the wrap. Fold the bottom point up and over the filling and roll up
tightly. When you reach the middle, fold in the corners from either side and brush
a little of the cornflour mixture onto the remaining corner. Finish rolling and seal
by pressing the edge. Do the same with the remaining mixture and wrappers.

Fill a deep saucepan with oil and heat to 180°C/350°F. It's ready when a cube
of bread turns golden in about 20 seconds. Deep-fry the spring rolls in batches
for 2–3 minutes, until golden brown and crispy. Put on a plate lined with kitchen
paper and sprinkle with a little salt. Serve immediately.

野菜のボブん　　VEGETARIAN NOODLE BOWL

Serves
4

300g (10½oz) rice noodles

½ cos lettuce, shredded

¼ small cucumber (around
150g/5oz/1 cup), chopped

small handful freshly shredded mint

small handful freshly shredded
coriander

1 small carrot, coarsely grated

100g (3½oz/⅔ cup) edamame
beans, defrosted

1 small mild red chilli, deseeded and
finely sliced (optional – add if you
want extra spice)

20g (¾oz) ready-made fried onions

40g (1½oz) roasted or salted
peanuts, finely chopped

❋ FOR THE GINGER TERIYAKI SAUCE

3 tbsp soy sauce

75g (3oz) caster sugar

15g (½oz) ginger purée or paste

❋ FOR THE TOFU

275g (9½oz/1½ cups) firm tofu,
drained and pressed (see tip on
page 70)

cornflour, to coat

sea salt

vegetable oil, to shallow-fry

8 spring rolls (see recipe and tips on
page 57) or use good-quality ready-
made rolls, cut into pieces

**There are lots of elements to this recipe, but it's well worth making
them all. The ginger teriyaki sauce can be made and chilled in advance
and the vegetables can be prepped earlier, while the spring rolls can be
made and chilled or frozen.**

First make the sauce. Pour the soy sauce and sugar into a small pan and stir in
the ginger purée or paste and 2 tablespoons cold water. Heat gently to dissolve
the sugar, stirring occasionally, then bring to the boil. Lower the heat and let the
sauce bubble for 6–7 minutes, until reduced slightly and thickened. Turn off the
heat and set aside to cool.

Next, prepare the pressed tofu. Cut it into about 2cm (¾in) cubes (around 10 per
serving). Put about 4 tablespoons of cornflour into a shallow dish and season
with salt. Add the tofu in small batches and gently toss to coat, patting off any
excess. Line a large plate with kitchen paper.

Pour enough oil into a heavy-based pan or wok until it is about 3–4cm (1¼–1½in)
deep and heat over a medium heat. It's ready when a cube of bread turns golden
in about 20 seconds.

Carefully lower the tofu into the hot oil – in small batches to ensure the pieces
don't stick together – and fry for 3–4 minutes until golden, stirring occasionally
with a slotted spoon. Lift out with a slotted spoon and drain on the lined plate.
Season with a little salt and keep warm.

Cook the rice noodles, following the instructions on the pack.

Divide the noodles among four bowls or lunch boxes, then layer the ingredients
on top starting with the lettuce, cucumber, mint, coriander, carrot and edamame
beans, followed by a few slices of chilli, if using.

Sprinkle over the fried onions and peanuts, then tuck the pieces of spring roll and
the tofu down the side.

Drizzle over the ginger teriyaki sauce and serve straightaway. If you're packing
this up for lunch, divide the sauce between four small containers and pack with
the salad.

春巻き

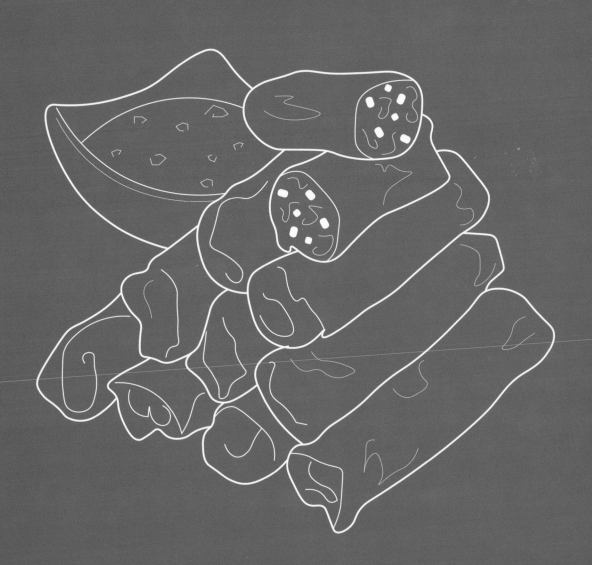

豆腐のボブん　　*TOFU WOK BOWL*

300g (10½oz) rice noodles

½ quantity of Mixed Vegetable
  Curry (see page 64)

40g (1½oz/⅓ cup) roasted or salted
  peanuts, finely chopped

small handful freshly chopped
  coriander

1 small mild red chilli, deseeded and
  finely sliced

✽ FOR THE TOFU

275g (9½oz/1½ cups) firm tofu,
  drained and pressed (see tip on
  page 70)

cornflour, to coat

sea salt

vegetable oil, to shallow-fry

✽ FOR THE SWEET AND SOUR SAUCE

3 tbsp soy sauce

1¾ tbsp lemon juice (approximately
  ½ large lemon), strained

50g (2oz) caster sugar

½ tsp sesame oil

With all its unique elements, this is a show-stopping dish. The tofu is chopped into Asian-style chunky tofu chips and they're served alongside rice noodles and a creamy coconut curry, drizzled with a moreish sweet and sour sauce.

Make the sweet and sour sauce. Pour the soy sauce, lemon juice and caster sugar into a bowl and stir together to help the sugar to dissolve. Stir in the sesame oil and set aside while the sugar dissolves gradually.

Prepare the pressed tofu. Cut it into 12 oblongs, each about 7 x 2cm (2¾ x ¾in). Put 2 tablespoons of cornflour into a shallow dish and season with salt. Add the tofu a few pieces at a time. Gently toss to coat all the pieces, patting off any excess. Line a large plate with kitchen paper.

Pour enough oil into a wok or heavy-based pan until it is about 3–4cm (1¼–1½in) deep and heat over a medium heat. It's ready when a cube of bread turns golden in about 20 seconds.

Carefully lower the tofu into the hot oil – in two batches, so the tofu doesn't overcrowd the pan and stick together. Fry for about 4 minutes until golden, stirring occasionally with a slotted spoon. Lift out with a slotted spoon and drain on the lined plate. Season with a little salt and keep warm.

Cook the rice noodles, following the instructions on the pack. Warm up the mixed vegetable curry if you have made it ahead.

Divide the rice noodles among four bowls. Top one side with an even portion of the tofu and the other side with the curry. Sprinkle over the peanuts, coriander and chilli.

Pour the sauce into a bowl to spoon over and serve.

野菜カレー　　　*MIXED VEGETABLE CURRY*

Serves
4

about 3 tbsp sunflower oil

½ small red onion, sliced

2 heaped tbsp Thai red curry paste

1 small sweet potato, around 160g
(5½oz/1 cup), chopped into 2cm
(¾in) cubes

175g (6oz/1 cup) piece butternut
squash, chopped into 2cm (¾in)
cubes

½ red pepper, deseeded and thickly
sliced

1 small courgette, sliced into 1cm
(½in) thick rounds

½ small broccoli head, cut into small
florets and stems chopped

50g (2oz/⅔ cup) shiitake mushrooms,
sliced

100ml (3½fl oz/scant ½ cup) hot
vegetable stock

400ml (14fl oz) can coconut milk

2 fresh lime leaves, shredded, or use
freeze-dried leaves if you can't get
hold of fresh

2 sprigs Thai basil, leaves picked and
roughly torn

sea salt and freshly ground black
pepper

This recipe makes double the quantity for the tofu wok bowl, but keeps well in the fridge for up to three days. Reheat in a pan with a splash of water when you come to eat it again.

Heat 1 tablespoon of the oil in a teppan, a wok or large frying pan over a medium-high heat. Once the oil is hot and shimmers, stir in the red onion and curry paste. Stir-fry for 2 minutes.

Add another 1 tablespoon oil, then the sweet potato and squash and stir-fry for a further 5 minutes to soften the vegetables.

Add the red pepper, courgette and broccoli. Season well and stir-fry for 3 minutes. Stir in the mushrooms and briefly stir-fry until the mushrooms start to wilt. If using a teppan, scoop the vegetables into a saucepan and place over a medium heat.

Pour in the stock and coconut milk and add the lime leaves. Bring to the boil. Turn the heat down and simmer for 8–9 minutes, uncovered, to thicken the sauce and finish cooking the vegetables, stirring occasionally. Stir in the basil and remove from the heat and serve.

炒飯   *CLASSIC STIR-FRIED RICE*

300g (10½oz/1½ cups) sushi rice
3 tbsp seasoned vinegar for sushi rice
3 tbsp vegetable oil
1 medium carrot, diced
4 eggs, beaten
1 tsp vegetable stock powder,
     dissolved in 2 tbsp boiling water
160g (5½oz) can sweetcorn, drained
120g (4½oz/¾ cup) frozen peas,
     defrosted
sea salt

We've included instructions on how to prepare the rice, but this will turn into a meal-in-minutes if you have cooked rice in the fridge. You can rustle up a batch when you're cooking other meals (you can store it in the fridge for up to a day). It's important to fry off the carrot for a few minutes first, so don't skip this stage.

Pour the rice into a sieve and rinse well. Tip into a saucepan and pour over 500ml (18fl oz/generous 2 cups) water. Stir in ½ teaspoon salt. Cover the pan and bring to the boil. As soon as the water boils, turn the heat down to low and simmer for 10 minutes. Set the pan aside off the heat, without taking the lid off and let it stand for 10 minutes.

Spoon the rice onto a plate, drizzle over the seasoned vinegar and stir it in.

Heat a drizzle of the oil on a teppan or in a large wok or large frying pan over a medium-high heat. As soon as the oil has heated through and easily coats the base of the pan, add the carrot and cook for 2–3 minutes until it's starting to soften. Remove to a plate and set aside.

Add the remaining oil to the pan and add the beaten eggs. Stir the eggs so they cook in the heat of the pan, like scrambled eggs.

Stir in the rice, then add a pinch of salt and the vegetable stock and mix together.

Add the sweetcorn, peas and carrot and continue to stir-fry for about 2 minutes, until everything's heated through and the carrot is tender.

Taste to check the seasoning, then serve.

野菜たっぷり
チャーハン

STIR-FRIED RICE WITH VEGETABLES

300g (10½oz/1½ cups) sushi rice

3 tbsp seasoned vinegar for sushi rice

2 tbsp vegetable oil

180g (6oz/2½ cups) carrot, sliced into matchsticks

180g (6oz/2¼ cups) chestnut or shiitake mushrooms, thinly sliced

80g (3oz/½ cup) mangetout

80g (3oz/½ cup) frozen peas, defrosted

2 spring onions, thinly sliced

salt

✽ FOR THE FRIED RICE SAUCE

100g (3½oz/½ cup) caster sugar

225ml (8fl oz/1 cup) oyster sauce or vegetarian oyster sauce

5 tbsp soy sauce

1 tbsp yakisoba sauce (omit if vegetarian)

This is an absolute classic and very easy to put together. Although it can be eaten just as it is, it also makes a great side dish, alongside chicken katsu or with a couple of spring rolls, if you have any stored in the freezer. For vegetarians, use vegetarian 'oyster' sauce instead and leave out the yakisoba sauce.

First, make the fried rice sauce. Put all the ingredients into a pan and heat gently to dissolve the sugar, stirring occasionally, until you can no longer feel the grains of sugar against the sides of the pan. Bring to the boil, then take off the heat. Once completely cool, this can be stored in a sealed bottle in the fridge for up to five days.

Pour the rice into a sieve and rinse well. Tip into a saucepan and pour over 500ml (18fl oz/generous 2 cups) water. Stir in ½ teaspoon salt. Cover and bring to the boil. As soon as the water is boiling, turn the heat down to low and simmer for 10 minutes. Set the pan aside off the heat, without taking the lid off, and let it stand for 10 minutes.

Spoon the rice onto a plate, drizzle over the seasoned vinegar and stir it in.

Heat a teppan or a large, flat frying pan over a medium heat until hot. Drizzle in 1 tablespoon of the vegetable oil. Set aside a small handful of the carrot, then add the remainder to the pan with the mushrooms and mangetout. Stir-fry until tender and the mangetout have turned bright green and are still a little crisp. Remove to a plate and set aside. Add another 1 tablespoon oil to the pan.

Put the cooked fried rice onto the teppan or into the frying pan and drizzle over 4 tablespoons fried rice sauce and stir to mix. Cook for a couple of minutes until heated through.

Return the mushrooms, carrot and mangetout to the pan with the peas and continue to stir-fry until everything is heated through. Season to taste.

Divide among four bowls and scatter over the spring onions and the reserved carrot.

チキンカツの味噌うどん

CHICKEN KATSU NOODLES

2 tbsp vegetable oil

400g (14oz/5 cups) wedge white cabbage, any hard core removed, finely sliced

2 spring onions, sliced

½ red pepper, deseeded and finely sliced

4 x 150g (5oz) portions straight-to-wok udon noodles

4 tbsp teriyaki sauce

salt and freshly ground black pepper

❋ FOR THE CHICKEN KATSU

2 large skinless, boneless chicken breasts

cornflour, to coat

1 egg

7–8 tbsp panko breadcrumbs

sunflower or vegetable oil, for shallow-frying

❋ FOR THE MISO SAUCE (MAKES DOUBLE)

50g (2oz) white miso

50g (2oz) caster sugar

1 tbsp honteri mirin

30g (1¼oz) sesame seeds

15g (½oz) neri goma (black sesame paste)

1 fat garlic clove, crushed

2½ tbsp soy sauce

> **TIP**
> Store the remaining quantity of miso sauce in the fridge and use within five days.

There's lots of wonderful textures to this recipe from the crunchy strips of crispy chicken katsu to the silky udon noodles. The miso sauce combines nutty sesame seeds, salty soy and miso, plus a dash of mirin for a touch of acidity. Use the Middle Eastern sesame paste, tahini, if you can't get hold of the Japanese version, neri goma.

First make the miso sauce. Put all the ingredients in a bowl and stir together until combined. Set aside.

Next, make the chicken katsu. Put the chicken breasts on a board and slice each one horizontally through the middle into two thin pieces. Lay between two sheets of clingfilm and bash with a rolling pin to flatten until they're around 1cm (½in) thick.

Spoon about 2 tablespoons cornflour into a shallow dish. Beat the egg in another separate dish and put the breadcrumbs into another. Dip the chicken pieces first in the cornflour (patting off any excess), then in the egg and then in the breadcrumbs until they're coated all over.

Heat 1–2 tablespoons oil in a large, flat frying pan over a medium-high heat. Fry the chicken pieces, in batches if necessary, until golden on one side (about 4–5 minutes), then turn over and fry on the other side until golden, about 4–5 minutes. Check the chicken is cooked – it should no longer be pink in the middle. Lift out onto a plate, sprinkle with a little salt and keep warm.

Heat the 2 tablespoons oil on the teppan or in a large, flat frying pan. As soon as the oil is hot and looks as though it's shimmering, add the cabbage, spring onions and red pepper. Stir-fry for 3–4 minutes on a high heat, until the veg are starting to turn tender. Lower the heat to medium.

Add the noodles to the cabbage mix, stir to break them up, sprinkle with 1–2 tablespoons cold water and season well. Drizzle over half the miso sauce (see tip) and half the teriyaki sauce, then continue to cook, tossing every few minutes until everything is heated through.

Slice each of the cooked chicken breasts on a board into 6 pieces.

To serve, divide the noodle mixture between four bowls and top with the chicken, then drizzle over the remaining teriyaki sauce.

STIR-FRIED NOODLES WITH TOFU

豆腐焼きそば

Serves 4

275g (9½oz/1½ cups) firm tofu, drained and pressed (see tip on page 70)
cornflour, to coat
sea salt
vegetable oil, to shallow-fry

✽ FOR THE NOODLES

250g (9oz/4 nests) medium dried egg noodles
3 tbsp vegetable oil, plus extra to drizzle
100ml (3½ fl oz/scant ½ cup) oyster sauce or vegetarian oyster sauce
2 tbsp soy sauce
1 tsp vegetable stock powder, dissolved in 2 tbsp boiling water
½ small broccoli head, cut into florets
½ each red and yellow pepper, deseeded and thinly sliced
1 medium carrot, cut into batons
125g (4½oz/1⅔ cups) chestnut or shiitake mushrooms, sliced
2 spring onions, sliced
½ tsp freshly ground black pepper

TIP
To ensure the tofu is as crisp as possible, it needs to be pressed to remove any excess water. Line a plate with kitchen paper and put the drained tofu on top. Cover with another sheet of kitchen paper, then put a flat plate on top, followed by a weight (e.g. a can of beans) and leave for 15–30 minutes to drain.

These bite-size chunks of tofu are lightly fried to give them a crisp outer texture, which turns a humble egg noodle stir-fry into something special. You can use vegetarian 'oyster' sauce, which uses mushroom as its seasoning for a veggie meal.

Start by preparing the pressed tofu. Cut it into about 2cm (¾in) cubes – you should end up with around 10 pieces per person. Put 4 tablespoons of cornflour into a shallow dish and season with salt. In batches, toss the tofu in the cornflour, patting off any excess, and place onto a plate.

Line a large plate with kitchen paper. Pour enough oil into a heavy-based pan or wok until it comes to a depth of about 3–4cm (1¼–1½in) and heat over a medium heat. It's ready when a cube of bread turns golden in about 20 seconds.

Carefully lower the tofu into the hot oil – in batches so the cubes of tofu are less likely to stick together – and fry for 3–4 minutes until golden, stirring occasionally with a slotted spoon. Lift out with a slotted spoon and drain on the lined plate. Season with a little salt and keep warm.

Add the noodles to a pan of boiling water, cover, then take off the heat and leave for 4–5 minutes until tender, then drain. Return to the pan with a drizzle of vegetable oil to stop them from sticking together.

Mix together the oyster sauce, soy sauce and vegetable stock in a bowl.

Heat the vegetable oil on a teppan or in a large frying pan or wok. As soon as the oil has heated through and shimmers, add the broccoli, peppers, carrot and mushrooms to the pan. Stir-fry on a high heat for 3–4 minutes until the vegetables start to turn tender.

Reduce the heat, then pour the oyster sauce mixture over the stir-fried vegetables. Stir-fry until all the vegetables are coated in the sauce.

Add the noodles and spring onions and season with the black pepper. Toss everything together again, add a few spoonfuls of water if it looks a little dry. Cook for a few more minutes to heat through. Divide among four bowls, top with the tofu and serve.

チキンチャーハン

STIR-FRIED RICE WITH CHICKEN

Serves
4

300g (10½oz/1½ cups) sushi rice

3 tbsp seasoned vinegar for sushi rice

1½ tbsp vegetable oil

1 large carrot, finely shredded

100g (3½oz/⅔ cup) frozen peas, defrosted

325g (11½oz/2⅓ cups) leftover cooked chicken, cut into cubes

2 spring onions, thinly sliced

sea salt and freshly ground black pepper

✾ FOR THE FRIED RICE SAUCE (SEE TIP)

100g (3½oz/½ cup) caster sugar

220ml (8fl oz/1 cup) oyster sauce

80ml (3fl oz/⅓ cup) soy sauce

1 tbsp yakisoba sauce

Here's the perfect recipe to cook on a Monday night if you have leftover chicken from a Sunday roast. It can also be adapted to whatever leftover roast meat you have to hand. The sauce makes more than is needed and can be used in the Stir-fried Rice with Vegetables recipe (see page 66), too.

Pour the rice into a sieve and rinse well. Tip into a saucepan and pour over 500ml (18 fl oz/generous 2 cups) water. Stir in ½ teaspoon salt. Cover and bring to the boil. As soon as the water is boiling, turn the heat down to low and simmer for 10 minutes. Set the pan aside off the heat, without taking the lid off and let it stand for 10 minutes.

Spoon the rice onto a plate, drizzle over the seasoned vinegar and stir it in.

Put all the fried rice sauce ingredients into a pan and heat gently to dissolve the sugar, stirring occasionally. It has dissolved when you can no longer feel the grains of sugar against the sides of the pan. Bring to the boil, then take off the heat. Once completely cool, this can be stored in the fridge in a sealed bottle for up to five days.

Mix the cooked rice with 4 tablespoons of the fried rice sauce.

Heat a teppan or a large, flat frying pan over a medium heat and drizzle in 1 tablespoon of the oil. Set aside a handful of the shredded carrot, then add the remainder to the pan and fry for 2 minutes to soften. Add the rice mixture, along with the peas and fry, stirring until thoroughly mixed and heated through.

Season well and stir everything together. Keep warm on a low heat.

Mix the chicken with 2–3 tablespoons of the fried rice sauce – just enough to coat the pieces. Heat a separate frying pan over a medium heat (or use another part of the teppan if there's enough room) and drizzle in the remaining vegetable oil. Once the oil is hot, quickly pan-fry the chicken to heat through.

Divide the rice among four bowls, top with the chicken and garnish with the spring onions and the reserved carrot and serve.

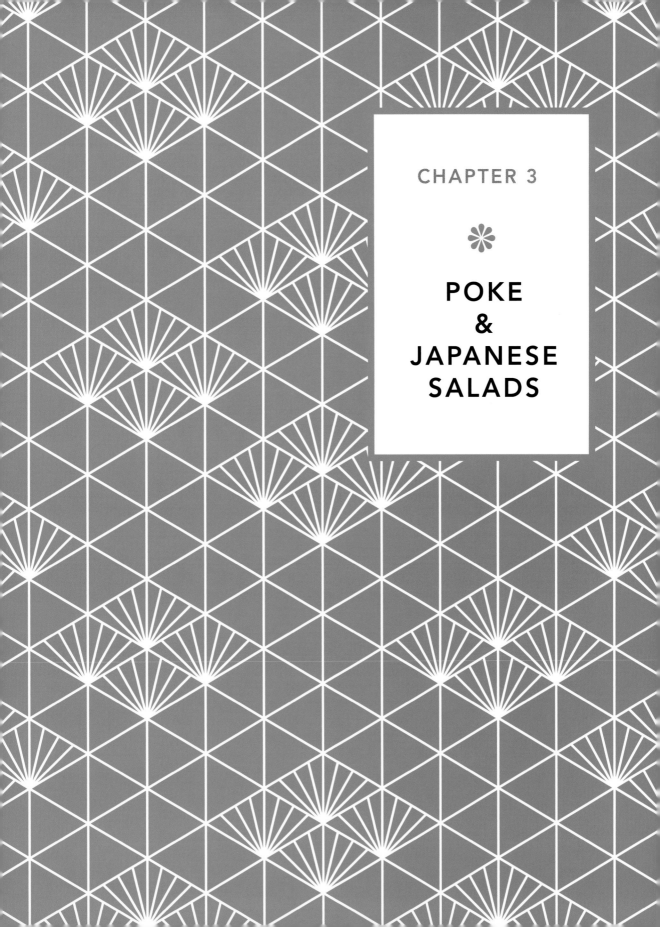

CHAPTER 3

❋

POKE
&
JAPANESE
SALADS

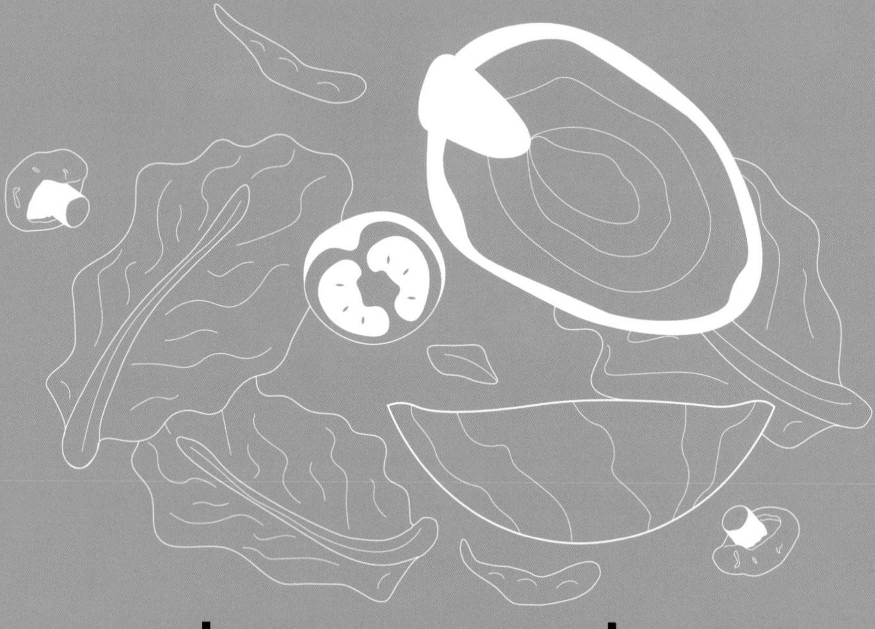

舌が肥える

shita ga koeru

——

Someone who has eaten many types of food
and has a discerning palate.

A balance of simple ingredients lies at the heart of these recipes with plenty of colour to boot. The soft summer rolls, so called because they enclose fresh, summery ingredients in a rice paper wrap, are a mash-up of salad and sandwich. The rice paper is dried, so keeps for ages in the cupboard. It just needs a quick dunk in a bowl of warm water to soften it enough to use. Fill them with finely chopped salad and shredded meat, fish or tofu but get the bits prepped first so you're ready to roll (excuse the pun!). Everything needs to be chopped in similar sizes so that once they're wrapped the vegetables are like pieces in a jigsaw and all fit together quite tightly. Match with a pot of sweet chilli sauce – this is the dressing – to dip into.

For a more traditional bowl of salad, go for a teriyaki salad or poke (*poh-kay*) bowl, where a bed of seasoned sushi rice forms the base. For the former, the protein (meat, fish or tofu) is quickly stir-fried in teriyaki marinade to contrast with the simple rice and refreshing salad.

Poke bowls were invented by Hawaiian fishermen who used to enjoy offcuts from their catch, seasoned to their tastes. The recipes developed into beautiful bowls of salad where everything is carefully prepared and cut into similar sizes. The height of it all in a bowl is important as is each ingredient being portioned separately so you can see exactly what it consists of. Just as in Japanese cooking, there's a deep respect for everything that's enjoyed. For these recipes, we've added our own twists and Japanese-inspired additions, and we're sure they'll become firm favourites.

海老とマンゴーの
生春巻き

PRAWN AND MANGO
CRYSTAL ROLLS

Serves
4

16 cooked and peeled tiger prawns

8 x 22cm (8½in) rounds Vietnamese
   rice paper (or use 12 x 16cm/6¼in
   rounds; see tip)

½ small mango, sliced into long strips

½ red pepper, deseeded and finely
   sliced

½ yellow pepper, deseeded and
   finely sliced

3cm (1¼in) piece red cabbage,
   finely sliced into batons (around
   50g/2oz/⅔ cup)

½ small carrot, cut into thin batons

4cm (1½in) piece Chinese cabbage,
   finely sliced into thin strips

16 mint leaves

❀ TO SERVE

sweet chilli sauce

Fish and fruit may seem like an odd combination – until you try these rolls. The mango enhances the fish and sweetens the salad in these rice paper wraps. You'll need to devein the prawns first: just slide the blade down the back to open it up and scrape away the black vein inside.

Take a prawn and use a small, sharp knife to slice through the back. Carefully remove and discard the vein. Slice almost all the way through, but keep part of it attached, so you can open it out into a butterfly. Do the same with the remaining prawns.

Fill a large bowl with warm water – it should be tepid but not too hot. Take a round of rice paper and dip it into the bowl for 5–20 seconds, depending on how warm the water is (see tip). It's ready when it feels slightly floppy and silky when you pull it out of the water and the time will depend on the temperature of the water. Make sure that it doesn't soften so much that it breaks up – it will soften more out of the water.

Lay the round on a board and place 2 prawns on top, end to end, around a third of the way down, leaving a 2.5cm (1in) border each side. Add a couple of strips of mango, horizontally, around two-thirds of the way down the round. Fill with a little red and yellow pepper, some red cabbage, carrot batons and Chinese cabbage. Lay a couple of mint leaves on top.

Wrap the bottom half of the round over the ingredients and roll up tightly, folding in the sides as you roll. Do the same again with the other rice paper rounds.

Serve two rolls per person, with a little pot of sweet chilli sauce to dip into.

> ## TIP
> If you've never made a crystal roll before, working with the slippery, softened rice paper can be tricky. If the paper is sticking to your board, line the board with a lightly dampened tea towel. The smaller, 16cm (6¼in) rice paper rounds need less time.
>
> Finely slice all the vegetables into very similar sizes. They should fit together like the pieces in a jigsaw so when you wrap them up, it makes a smooth roll.
>
> As you wrap more rolls up, leave them either on the edge of the damp tea towel, if you're using, or on a plate so that you can lift them up easily.

鶏肉ときゅうり の生春巻き

CHICKEN AND CUCUMBER CRYSTAL ROLLS

8 x 22cm (8½in) rounds Vietnamese rice paper (or use 12 x 16cm/6¼in rounds; see tip on page 76)

1 x quantity cooked Chicken Teriyaki Salad, chopped (see page 90)

5cm- (2in-) long piece cucumber, halved lengthways, deseeded and cut into 16 thin baton-length pieces

½ red pepper, deseeded and finely sliced

½ yellow pepper, deseeded and finely sliced

3–4cm (1¼–1½in) piece daikon radish, cut into thin batons (or use 8 radishes, chopped)

1 small carrot, cut into thin batons

50–80g (2–3oz/⅔–1 cup) wedge of iceberg or Little Gem lettuce, finely sliced

16 mint leaves

❋ **TO SERVE**

sweet chilli sauce

A sort-of Asian equivalent of a chicken sandwich – chicken teriyaki is rolled up with a chopped salad and wrapped in rice paper. Make double the quantity for the chicken teriyaki (see page 90) and you'll have enough to make this and the salad, too. If you want to use leftover roast chicken, just toss it first in a little teriyaki marinade.

Fill a large bowl with warm water – it should be tepid but not too hot.

Take a round of rice paper, dip it into the bowl and leave it in there long enough to soften. It's ready when it feels slightly floppy and silky when you pull it out of the water. Depending on the temperature of the water it will take anything from 5–20 seconds. Make sure that it doesn't soften so much that it breaks up. It needs to feel just flexible as it will soften more once out of the water.

Lay the round on a board and place around an eighth of the chicken on top and 2 strips of cucumber, horizontally, about two-thirds of the way down the round. Fill with a little red and yellow pepper, some radish, carrot and lettuce, leaving about 2.5cm (1in) either side of the round (so when you roll, the filling does not fall out). Lay a couple of mint leaves on top.

Wrap the bottom half of the round over the ingredients and roll up tightly, folding in the sides as you roll. Do the same again with the other rice paper rounds to make eight rolls.

Serve two rolls per person, with a little pot of sweet chilli sauce to dip into.

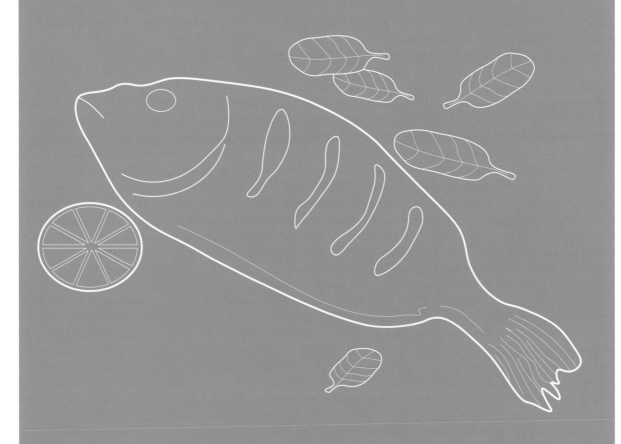

サーモンとアボカドの生春巻き

SALMON AND AVOCADO CRYSTAL ROLLS

Serves
4

8 x 22cm (8½in) rounds Vietnamese
rice paper (or use 12 x 16cm/6¼in
rounds; see tip on page 76)
4 x 70g (2½oz) pieces skinned very
fresh or sashimi-grade salmon (see
page 17), sliced into finger-length
pieces
1 large avocado, stoned, peeled and
finely sliced
½ red pepper, deseeded and finely
sliced
½ yellow pepper, deseeded and
finely sliced
3cm (1¼in) piece red cabbage,
finely sliced
1 small carrot, cut into thin batons
around 70g (2½oz/1 cup) iceberg or
Little Gem lettuce, finely sliced
16 mint leaves

✽ TO SERVE
sweet chilli sauce

The firm, succulent texture of raw salmon really makes these stand out, especially with slivers of creamy avocado tucked in. Go easy on the sweet chilli dipping sauce, so you don't overpower the overall bite.

Fill a large bowl with warm water – it should be tepid but not too hot.

Take a round of rice paper, dip it into the bowl and leave it in there long enough to soften. It's ready when it feels slightly floppy and silky when you pull it out of the water. Depending on the temperature of the water, this will take anything from 5–20 seconds. Make sure that it doesn't soften so much that it breaks up – it will soften more out of the water.

Lay the round on a board and place around an eighth of the salmon on top and 2 slices of avocado, horizontally, around two-thirds of the way down the round, leaving a 2.5cm (1in) border. Fill with a little red and yellow pepper, some red cabbage, carrot and lettuce. Lay a couple of mint leaves on top.

Wrap the bottom half of the round over the ingredients and roll up tightly, folding in the sides as you roll. Do the same again with the other rice paper rounds.

Serve 2 rolls per person, with a little pot of sweet chilli sauce to dip into to.

ホノルルポキ丼　　*HONOLULU POKE*

Serves
4

300g (11oz/1½ cups) sushi rice

½ tsp salt

3 tbsp seasoned vinegar for sushi rice

4 x 70–80g (2½–3oz) pieces very fresh or sashimi-grade salmon (see page 17), chopped

80g (3oz/½ cup) edamame beans, fresh or frozen and defrosted

½ large mango, stoned, peeled and chopped

2 tbsp ready-made fried onions

❋ **FOR THE PICKLED RED CABBAGE**

2 tbsp rice wine vinegar

½ tsp salt

1 tsp caster sugar

¼ medium red cabbage (around 200g/7oz/2⅔ cups), diced or finely sliced

❋ **FOR THE POKE DRESSING**

3 tbsp dark soy sauce

2 tbsp honteri mirin

2 tbsp rice wine vinegar

1½ tsp sesame oil

½ tsp yuzu juice

See photograph overleaf.

The pickled red cabbage provides an eye-catching punch of colour here, alongside the salmon and edamame beans. It's the perfect late-summer supper, when it's still warm outside and you're hankering after something healthy.

Place the rice in a sieve and rinse well. Put into a saucepan and pour over 500ml (18fl oz/generous 1 cup) water. Stir in the salt. Cover the pan and bring to the boil, then turn the heat down to the lowest setting and simmer for around 10 minutes. Turn off the heat and, without taking the lid off, set aside for 10 minutes.

To make the pickled red cabbage, mix the vinegar, salt and sugar together in a non-reactive bowl, then add the red cabbage. Toss everything together and set aside for 10 minutes so that the vinegar pickles the cabbage.

To make the poke dressing, put the soy sauce into a bowl, add the mirin, vinegar, sesame oil and yuzu juice and whisk together.

As soon as the rice is cooked, spoon it onto a plate and pour over the seasoned vinegar. Stir it in, then spread the rice into an even layer and leave to cool.

Divide the rice among four bowls. Top each with a portion of salmon and a portion each of pickled red cabbage, edamame beans and mango. Drizzle the poke dressing over the top and finish by sprinkling over the fried onions.

ヒロポキ丼　　　*HILO POKE*

300g (10½oz/1½ cups) sushi rice

½ tsp salt

240g (9oz/¾ cup) small cooked, peeled prawns, defrosted if frozen (around 600g/1¼lb unpeeled weight)

1 tbsp teriyaki marinade

3 tbsp seasoned vinegar for sushi rice

100g (3½oz/⅔ cup) edamame beans, fresh or frozen and defrosted

½ small mango, diced

1 tsp each black and toasted white sesame seeds

✿ FOR THE PICKLED RED ONION

1 tbsp rice wine vinegar

½ tsp caster sugar

¼ tsp salt

½ small red onion, finely sliced

✿ FOR THE POKE DRESSING

3 tbsp dark soy sauce

2 tbsp honteri mirin

2 tbsp rice wine vinegar

1½ tsp sesame oil

½ tsp yuzu juice

There's a terrific range of good-quality frozen seafood available now in supermarkets, handy for rustling up these kinds of recipes. The small north Atlantic prawns which are already cooked (but may need to be peeled first) are perfect for this and just need tossing in a little marinade to season first.

Place the rice in a sieve and rinse well. Put into a saucepan and pour over 500ml (18fl oz/generous 2 cups) water. Stir in the salt. Cover the pan and bring to the boil, then turn the heat down to the lowest setting and simmer for around 10 minutes. Lift the pan off the heat and set aside, without taking the lid off, for 10 minutes.

Meanwhile, toss the prawns and teriyaki marinade together in a bowl and set aside to marinate.

To pickle the red onion, put the rice wine vinegar, caster sugar and salt into a bowl and stir in the red onion. Set the bowl aside – 5–10 minutes is long enough for the vinegar to pickle the onion.

Once the rice is cooked, spoon it onto a plate and pour over the seasoned vinegar. Stir it in, then spread the rice into an even layer and leave to cool.

Divide the rice among four bowls and top with a portion of the marinated prawns and a portion each of the edamame beans, mango and pickled red onion.

Whisk all the ingredients for the poke dressing together in a small bowl and spoon over the top of the bowls, then sprinkle over the sesame seeds.

チキンポキ丼

CHICKEN POKE

300g (10½oz/1½ cups) wild rice mix
(a combination of wild rice, red rice
and long-grain rice)

½ tsp salt

1 small carrot, coarsely grated

100g (3½oz/⅔ cup) edamame
beans, fresh or frozen and
defrosted

3 tbsp mixed seeds (sunflower,
pumpkin and sesame seeds),
toasted if you like

❋ FOR THE RED CABBAGE SALAD

2 tbsp rice wine vinegar

½ tsp caster sugar

½ tsp salt

160g (5½oz/2 cups) red cabbage,
finely sliced

❋ FOR THE CHICKEN KATSU

1 large skinless, boneless chicken
breast (around 200g/7oz)

1–2 tbsp cornflour, to coat

1 medium egg

25–30g (1–1¼oz/¼–⅔ cup) panko
breadcrumbs

vegetable oil, to shallow-fry

salt

❋ FOR THE POKE DRESSING

3 tbsp dark soy sauce

2 tbsp honteri mirin

2 tbsp rice wine vinegar

1½ tsp sesame oil

½ tsp yuzu juice

The combination of textures from the crisp-fried chicken katsu, crunchy vegetables, quick-pickled cabbage and tender rice is what makes this salad shine. The wild rice mix brings a delicious nutty flavour, but if you can't get hold of it, use a long-grain and wild rice mix instead.

Place the rice in a sieve and rinse well. Put into a saucepan and pour over 750ml (1⅓ pints/scant 3 cups) water. Stir in the salt. Cover the pan and bring to the boil, then turn the heat down to the lowest setting and simmer for around 30 minutes. Lift the pan off the heat and set aside for 10 minutes, without lifting the lid.

While the rice is cooking, make the red cabbage salad. Put the vinegar, sugar and salt into a medium bowl and stir together. Add the red cabbage and mix well. Set aside to marinate for 5–10 minutes.

Next, make the chicken katsu. Line a large plate with kitchen paper and a large board with clingfilm. Place the chicken breast, smooth-side down on the board. Open out the tenderloin (the extra piece of chicken that sits underneath the breast) so the piece lies flat. Cover with another piece of clingfilm. Use a rolling pin to flatten the pieces until they're around ½cm (¼in) thick. Cut each in half widthways to make four pieces.

Spoon the cornflour into a shallow dish. Put the egg into another dish and beat with a little salt. Place the breadcrumbs in another dish. Dip the chicken pieces first in the cornflour (patting off any excess), then in the egg and then in the breadcrumbs until they're coated all over.

Heat just enough oil to coat the bottom of a large, flat frying pan over a medium-high heat. It's ready when you drop a little piece of breadcrumb in and it starts to sizzle. Fry the chicken pieces, in batches if necessary, for about 3 minutes on one side until golden. Turn over and fry for about 2–3 minutes until golden and the chicken is cooked through. Lift out onto the lined plate, sprinkle with a little salt and keep warm.

Whisk all the ingredients for the dressing together. Divide the rice among four bowls. Slice the chicken into thin strips and place on top of the rice. Add a spoonful of the red cabbage, then the carrot, then the beans. Drizzle over some of the dressing (serve the rest separately), sprinkle with the seed mix and serve.

パシフィックポキ丼　　*PACIFIC POKE*

Serves

4

300g (11oz/1½ cups) sushi rice

½ tsp salt

3 tbsp seasoned vinegar for sushi rice

4 x 70–80g pieces very fresh or sashimi-grade salmon (see page 17), chopped

100g (3½oz/⅔ cup) edamame beans, fresh or frozen and defrosted

½ small mango, chopped

2 tbsp ready-made fried onions

a few sprigs of coriander, to garnish

❋ FOR THE PICKLED RED ONION

1 tbsp rice wine vinegar

½ tsp caster sugar

¼ tsp salt

½ small red onion, finely sliced

❋ FOR THE WHITE CABBAGE SALAD

3 tbsp rice wine vinegar

25g (1oz) caster sugar

2 tbsp sunflower oil

½ tsp sesame oil

1 tbsp Dijon mustard

¼ white cabbage, shredded

½ carrot, grated

❋ FOR THE POKE DRESSING

3 tbsp dark soy sauce

2 tbsp honteri mirin

2 tbsp rice wine vinegar

1½ tsp sesame oil

½ tsp yuzu juice

Our Japanese version of a creamy coleslaw is this white cabbage salad, which is cut with a little carrot for colour. The sugar and vinegar pickle the vegetable while the oils and mustard combine to make an Asian-style mayo. It will keep for up to five days in the fridge. There's a little bit of heat from the mustard but it doesn't mask the delicacy of the raw salmon it's served with.

Place the rice in a sieve and rinse well. Put into a saucepan and pour over 500ml (18fl oz/generous 2 cups) water. Stir in the salt. Cover the pan and bring to the boil, then turn the heat down to the lowest setting and simmer for around 10 minutes. Set the pan aside off the heat, without taking the lid off, for 10 minutes.

Next, pickle the red onion by mixing the vinegar, caster sugar and salt together in a bowl, then stirring in the red onion. Set aside for 5–10 minutes.

Make the white cabbage salad. Pour the rice wine vinegar into a bowl and add the sugar, sunflower oil, sesame oil and mustard. Whisk well to combine. Add the cabbage and carrot and toss well.

Spoon the rice onto a plate and pour over the seasoned vinegar. Stir it in, then spread the rice into an even layer and leave to cool.

Divide the rice among four bowls. Top with a portion of the salmon, edamame beans and mango and then a portion each of the white cabbage salad and pickled red onion.

Whisk together all the ingredients for the poke dressing and pour over the top, then scatter over the fried onions and coriander.

豆腐の照り焼きサラダ

TOFU TERIYAKI SALAD

✱ FOR THE TERIYAKI TOFU

400g (14oz/2½ cups) firm tofu,
   pressed (see page 70) and cut into
   about 36 cubes
2 tbsp teriyaki marinade
sunflower or vegetable oil, for frying

✱ FOR THE SALAD

300g (10½oz/1½ cups) sushi rice
½ teaspoon salt
3 tbsp seasoned vinegar for sushi rice
100g (3½oz/⅔ cup) edamame
   beans, fresh or frozen and
   defrosted
½ red pepper, deseeded and thinly
   sliced
½ yellow pepper, deseeded and
   thinly sliced
8–12 cherry tomatoes, halved
4 radishes, halved through the root,
   cut into thin wedges
80–100g (3–3½oz/1–1⅓ cups)
   wedge of iceberg lettuce, chopped
1 tsp each black and toasted
   white sesame seeds
4 edible flowers, optional

✱ FOR THE DRESSING

3 tbsp teriyaki marinade
1 tsp sesame oil
1 tbsp Japanese mirin

Tofu is a great source of protein with a delicate taste and absorbs any seasoning it's paired with. It's pan-fried here with a dash of teriyaki – just enough to pack a hit of umami flavouring to work alongside the rice and vegetables.

Place the rice in a sieve and rinse under cold running water. Drain well. Tip into a saucepan then pour over 500ml (18fl oz/generous 2 cups) water, add the salt and bring to the boil. Cover the pan, lower the heat to the lowest setting and cook for 10 minutes. Set the pan aside off the heat and let it stand for 10 minutes, without lifting the lid.

Meanwhile, toss the tofu and the teriyaki marinade carefully together in a large, shallow bowl, so the tofu doesn't lose its shape. Heat a large frying pan with a drizzle of the oil until hot on a medium-high heat. Pan-fry the tofu pieces (half at a time if you need to cook in batches) with any marinade for about 3–4 minutes, until golden on all sides, turning frequently. Tip into a bowl with any juices and leave to cool.

Spoon the rice onto a large plate and pour over the seasoned vinegar. Stir it in, then spread the rice into an even layer and leave to cool.

Divide the rice among four bowls, then top with the teriyaki tofu and drizzle over any cooking juices.

Mix the edamame beans, peppers, tomatoes, radishes and lettuce together in a bowl. Divide among the four bowls (or arrange separately on plates).

Whisk the ingredients together for the dressing and drizzle over the salad. Sprinkle over the sesame seeds and top each with an edible flower, if you like, and serve.

CHICKEN TERIYAKI SALAD

Serves
4

✳ FOR THE CHICKEN TERIYAKI

400g (14oz) skinless, boneless
  chicken thighs, chopped into small
  pieces
3 tbsp teriyaki marinade
1.5cm (⅝in) piece of fresh root
  ginger, finely grated
sunflower or vegetable oil, for frying

✳ FOR THE SALAD

300g (10½oz/1½ cups) sushi rice
½ tsp salt
3 tbsp seasoned vinegar for sushi rice
100g (3½oz/⅔ cup) edamame
  beans, fresh or frozen and
  defrosted
½ red pepper, deseeded and
  chopped
½ yellow pepper, deseeded and
  chopped
3cm (1¼in) wide wedge red
  cabbage, finely sliced1 small carrot,
cut into thin batons
2 x 6cm (2½in) thick wedges iceberg
  lettuce, chopped
1 tsp each black and toasted
  white sesame seeds
4 edible flowers, optional

✳ FOR THE DRESSING

3 tbsp teriyaki marinade
1 tsp sesame oil
1 tbsp Japanese mirin

This is a really refreshing salad that is cooked in a teriyaki marinade for extra flavour. If you have leftover chicken and sushi rice already cooked and chilled, it can be rustled up in minutes. Just shred the cooked chicken and toss with a little teriyaki marinade. The salad should be crisp and crunchy when you eat it, so pour the dressing into a separate drip-proof container if you're packing it up for work.

Place the rice in a sieve and rinse under cold running water. Drain well. Tip into a saucepan, then pour over 500ml (18fl oz/generous 2 cups) water and add the salt. Cover the pan and bring to the boil, then turn the heat down to the lowest setting and simmer for around 10 minutes. Set the pan aside off the heat, without taking the lid off, for 10 minutes.

While the rice is cooking, prepare the chicken teriyaki. Put the chicken thighs into a non-metallic dish. Mix together the teriyaki marinade and ginger and pour over the chicken. Stir so that the chicken pieces are coated.

Heat a little oil in a large frying pan or wok on a high heat and as soon as the oil is hot, add half the chicken and stir-fry for 6–7 minutes until the chicken is cooked all the way through and any marinade in the pan has evaporated and coats the chicken. Spoon onto a plate, separate the pieces out and leave to cool. Continue cooking the rest of the chicken in the same way, adding a little more oil if needed.

Spoon the rice onto a large plate and pour over the seasoned vinegar. Stir it in, then spread the rice into an even layer and leave to cool.

Divide the rice among four bowls, then top with the teriyaki chicken.

Put the edamame beans, peppers, cabbage, carrot and lettuce into a bowl and mix together. Divide among the four bowls.

Whisk the ingredients together for the dressing and drizzle over the salad. Sprinkle over the sesame seeds and top each with an edible flower, if you like, and serve.

照り焼き
サーモンサラダ

SALMON TERIYAKI SALAD

✳ FOR THE TERIYAKI SALMON

400g (14oz) skinless salmon fillet,
  halved widthways

2 tbsp teriyaki marinade

sunflower or vegetable oil, for frying

✳ FOR THE SALAD

300g (10½oz/1½ cups) sushi rice

½ tsp salt

3 tbsp seasoned vinegar for sushi rice

100g (3½oz/⅔ cups) edamame
  beans, fresh or frozen and
  defrosted

½ red pepper, deseeded and
  chopped

½ yellow pepper, deseeded and
  chopped

100g (3½oz/⅔ cup) piece cucumber,
  halved lengthways, deseeded
  and thinly sliced

6 baby corn, sliced into quarters
  lengthways, then in half widthways

80–100g (3–3½oz/1–⅓ cups) wedge
  of iceberg lettuce, chopped

1 tsp each black and toasted
  white sesame seeds

4 edible flowers, optional

✳ FOR THE DRESSING

3 tbsp teriyaki marinade

1 tsp sesame oil

1 tbsp Japanese mirin

There's lots of ready-prepared cooked salmon, already marinated and
flavoured in supermarkets now, but pan-frying fresh, marinated salmon
gives it a moreish crust and means it flakes into delicate pieces.

Place the rice in a sieve and rinse under cold running water. Drain well. Tip into a
saucepan, then pour over 500ml (18fl oz/generous 2 cups) water and add the salt.
Cover the pan and bring to the boil, then turn the heat down to the lowest setting
and simmer for around 10 minutes. Set the pan aside off the heat and let it stand,
without lifting the lid, for 10 minutes.

Meanwhile, put the salmon into a non-metallic dish and pour over the teriyaki
marinade. Turn it over in the marinade to coat. Heat a little oil in a large, non-stick
frying pan over a medium heat. When the oil is hot, place the salmon in the pan,
skin-side down.

Lower the heat and cook for 3–5 minutes, until the salmon is almost cooked. Turn
over, pour over any marinade, and continue to cook for a further 1–2 minutes until
opaque all the way through. Lift out of the pan and onto a plate to cool, then flake
each piece into large flakes.

Spoon the rice onto a large plate and pour over the seasoned vinegar. Stir it in,
then spread the rice into an even layer and leave to cool.

Divide the rice among four bowls, then top each with a quarter of the teriyaki
salmon. Drizzle over any cooking juices from the pan.

Mix the edamame beans, peppers, cucumber, baby corn and lettuce together in
a bowl. Divide among the four bowls.

Whisk the ingredients together for the dressing and drizzle over the salad. Sprinkle
over the sesame seeds and top each with an edible flower, if you like, and serve.

椎茸

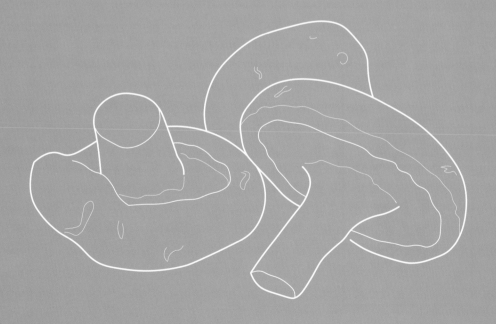

豆腐とキヌアの
シュウマイ

TOFU AND QUINOA SHUMAI

Makes
20

20 dumpling wrappers (see page 101)

❋ FOR THE FILLING

2 large dried shiitake
  mushrooms (around 6g/⅛oz/⅛ cup)

175g (6oz/1 cup) firm or extra firm
  tofu

50g (2oz/⅓ cup) cooked quinoa

1½ tbsp chopped green beans
  (about 3 green beans)

1 small spring onion, finely chopped,
  plus extra finely sliced to garnish,
  optional

¼ tsp salt

generous ½ tsp sugar

⅛ tsp ground white pepper

1½ tsp cornflour

2 tsp soy sauce

1 tsp sesame oil

2 tbsp finely diced carrot (around
  ¼ carrot)

❋ TO SERVE

soy sauce

Chinese hot mustard or Colman's
  English mustard

You'll also need a steamer, lined with
baking parchment.

These vegan bites also feature shiitake mushrooms and a smattering of spring onion and green beans. They're crowned with a spoonful of diced carrot to show them off. A simple bowl of soy sauce is great with these, but even better is a dab of punchy mustard.

Start by soaking the mushrooms for the filling in boiling water. Leave to soften for 10 minutes. Drain well and pat dry, then finely chop.

Prepare the rest of the filling. Gently squeeze the tofu to break it up and release some of the water. You don't have to make it totally dry. Put into a bowl, add the mushrooms, quinoa, beans and spring onion. Stir and lightly mash all the ingredients together until the tofu starts to crumble and everything is mixed well.

Put the salt into a small bowl and add the sugar, white pepper, cornflour, soy sauce and sesame oil. Whisk to combine, then pour over the tofu and quinoa mixture. Stir in the liquid, then use a fork or your hands to mash everything together.

Rest a dumpling wrapper between the thumb and forefinger of one hand. Scoop up about 1 tablespoon of filling into the centre of the wrapper, pressing it down gently. Gather the edge of the wrapper up and around the filling to create a border, pinching and folding into small pleats as you go, to give a round shape, with the filling exposed in the centre. It will be barrel-shaped and look like an open bag.

Set on a clean work surface or board to flatten the base. Spoon some finely diced carrot into the middle to finish it off. Set aside, spaced apart, on the baking parchment, covered with a dry tea towel or clingfilm, while you shape the rest.

Place the shumai in a steamer tray, open-side up, spacing them around 2–5cm (¾–2in) away from the edge, so they don't stick.

If you can't steam all the dumplings at once, steam in batches, keeping the uncooked ones covered to prevent them from drying out.

Steam the dumplings over a pan of boiling water for 6–8 minutes, until they have puffed slightly and their skins have become translucent. If you don't have a steamer, use the same technique on page 98. Remove each tray and place it on top of a serving plate. Serve immediately with the soy sauce and mustard.

餃子の皮　　*GYOZA WRAPPERS*

60–70ml (2¼–2½fl oz) just-boiled water
¼ tsp salt
120g (4½oz/1 cup) plain flour
cornflour, to dust

These simple wrappers are made from plain flour, water and salt, which are kneaded together to make a dough, rested, then shaped into rounds, ready to be filled. Easy!

Measure 60ml (2fl oz/¼ cup) of the water into a heatproof jug and add the salt. Stir to dissolve.

Sift the flour into a heatproof bowl and make a well in the middle. Pour the water gradually into the middle, stirring all the time.

Shape into a ball, scraping and mopping up all the flour from around the sides of the bowl as you do so. If it feels a bit dry, add the extra water to help the dough pick up and absorb any excess flour. Keep squeezing the mixture constantly until it starts to feel firm.

Transfer the ball to a clean work surface or board and knead for 10 minutes until very firm and until the skin of the dough no longer cracks. It should be very smooth.

Cut the dough in half and squeeze and roll each piece into a log, around 10cm (4in) in length. Wrap in clingfilm or in a sealable bag and set aside for 30 minutes at room temperature.

Cut one log into 10 even-sized pieces (each will be about 8g/¼oz). Cover the pieces with a damp tea towel to prevent them from drying out.

Take one piece of dough and shape it into a disc. Sprinkle the work surface or a board with a little cornflour and, using a rolling pin, roll out into a circle measuring 8cm (3¼in) – the wrapper should be around 1–2mm (less than ⅛in) thick. Dust with a little cornflour and put on a plate. Keep the dough covered with clingfilm until you're ready to use it.

Roll out the remaining pieces in the same way, then do the same again with the other log. If you end up with slightly odd-shaped rounds, use an 8cm- (¾in-) round scone cutter to neaten off.

TIP
Keep the wrappers covered as they're quite delicate and can dry out quickly.

餃子   *CLASSIC MEAT GYOZA*

Makes
20

2 dried shiitake mushrooms

50g (2oz/⅔ cup) Chinese cabbage, finely diced

½ tsp salt, plus a pinch

225g (8oz/1 cup) lean pork mince or chicken mince

5g (⅛in) garlic chives, finely chopped)

1½ tsp grated fresh root ginger (around 1–2cm/½–¾in piece)

1 tsp soy sauce

1 tsp sesame oil, plus extra for cooking

20 dumpling wrappers (see page 101)

1 nori half sheet, cut into very thin strips, to garnish

✳ FOR THE DIPPING SAUCE

2 tbsp soy sauce

2 tbsp rice wine vinegar

½ tsp La-yu (Japanese chilli oil), or to taste, optional

sesame seeds, to garnish

See photograph on pages 108–109.

> ### TIP
> You can make this filling mixture up to 2 days ahead and keep in the fridge.

If you can track down garlic chives, they will give a lovely herb and garlic flavour to the finished dumplings. If you can only buy regular chives, use the same quantity of herb and add 1 small crushed garlic clove to the mix, too.

Mix the sauce ingredients together. Sprinkle with sesame seeds and set aside.

Put the shiitake mushrooms into a bowl and pour over enough boiling water to cover. Soak for 10 minutes, then drain, finely chop and mop with kitchen paper to remove any excess liquid.

Put the cabbage into a bowl and sprinkle with the ½ tsp salt. Give it a bit of a massage and leave for 10–15 minutes. Drain well and squeeze out any excess moisture. Put the cabbage back into the bowl. Add the minced pork or chicken, the chives, the mushrooms, ginger, soy sauce, sesame oil and pinch of salt. Mix well.

Fill a small bowl with cold water. Dry your hands completely (or wrappers will stick). Rest a dumpling wrapper between the thumb and forefinger of one hand. Put 2 teaspoons of the filling into the middle and spread out slightly, leaving around 1cm (½in) border. Dip a finger in the water and run it around the edge of the wrapper. Make a semi-circle by folding the wrapper in half, pinching the nearest edge. Using your thumbs at the front of the wrapper, start to pleat the edge, keeping the back smooth and pushing the pleats against the back of the wrapper, lightly squeezing to secure and seal. Fill all the wrappers in this way.

Cook the dumplings in two batches. Heat 2 teaspoons sesame oil in a large frying pan over a medium heat. Fry the dumplings, flat-side down, for about 2 minutes until a golden crust forms on the bottom. Add 75ml (2½fl oz/⅓ cup) water and immediately cover with a lid and let the steam cook the dumplings for 8 minutes or until all the water has evaporated. Remove the lid and let the dumplings cook for another minute until they lift off from the bottom of the pan easily. You might need a spatula to help if they are a little sticky, being careful not to break the wrappers. Remove to a plate and keep hot. Repeat with the second batch.

Sprinkle the nori strips over the gyoza and serve hot with the dipping sauce.

102   餃子とシューマイ   GYOZA & DIM SUM

豚肉とキャベツの餃子

PORK AND CABBAGE GYOZA

Makes
20

20 dumpling wrappers (see recipe, page 101)
sunflower or vegetable oil, for cooking

✳ FOR THE FILLING

225g (8oz/3 cups) Chinese cabbage (about ¼ medium head), cut lengthways into long thin strips, then across to shred finely
½ tsp salt
225g (8oz/1 cup) pork mince
½ tsp ground white pepper
1 large garlic clove, crushed
1 tsp grated fresh root ginger, (around 1cm/½in piece)
1 spring onion, finely chopped

✳ FOR THE DIPPING SAUCE

4 tbsp rice wine vinegar
2 tbsp soy sauce
½–1 tsp chilli oil, depending on how hot you like it, optional

TIP

To make your own chilli oil, stir 2 large pinches chilli flakes into 4 tablespoons sunflower oil. Pour into a small jar and give it a good shake. Store in the cupboard. Remember to taste the oil before using as the longer you leave it, the hotter it becomes.

The beauty of this recipe is that it's made from just a handful of readily available ingredients. Chinese leaf cabbage, also known as Napa cabbage, gives a slightly sweet flavour here and provides body to the overall filling. Chilli oil works brilliantly in the sauce and there's a tip at the end of the recipe to make your own, too.

Stir all the dipping sauce ingredients together in a bowl and set aside.

Put the cabbage in a bowl and sprinkle over ¼ teaspoon of the salt. Give it a bit of a massage to rub the salt in and leave for 10–15 minutes. Squeeze the cabbage to remove any moisture, then drain well and pat dry.

Put the pork, drained cabbage, remaining salt, white pepper, garlic, ginger and spring onion in a large bowl and knead the mixture until it comes together and starts to feel slightly sticky and paste-like.

Fill a small bowl with cold water. Rest a dumping wrapper between your thumb and forefinger of one hand and place a heaped teaspoon of the pork mixture into the middle. Spread out slightly, leaving a border of around 1cm (½in). Dip a finger into the bowl of water and run it round the edge of the wrapper. Fold the wrapper in half to make a crescent shape.

Pinch the edge on one side of the wrapper to start to seal it. With your forefinger supporting the back of the wrapper, use your two thumbs to pleat the front of the wrapper. As you move along and start to shape the gyoza, keep pressing the front and back together with your forefinger and thumb. You'll end up with a curve of seven or eight pleats on the front of the gyoza and a smooth edge on the back. Fill all the wrappers in this way.

Cook the dumplings in two batches. Heat a little oil in a large frying pan over a medium heat. Fry the dumplings, flat-side down, for about 2 minutes until a golden crust forms on the bottom. Add 75ml (2½fl oz/⅓ cup) water and immediately cover the pan. Reduce the heat to low and cook the dumplings for 8 minutes or until all the water has evaporated. Take the lid off and let the dumplings cook for a further minute until they lift off the bottom of the pan easily. You might need a spatula to help them along if they are a little sticky, but take care not to break the wrappers. Repeat with the second batch of gyoza.

Serve hot with the dipping sauce.

エビ餃子　　　*PRAWN GYOZA*

Makes
20

20 dumpling wrappers (see page 101)

sunflower or vegetable oil, for frying

❋ FOR THE FILLING

100g (3½oz/1⅓ cups) Chinese,
  spring or Napa cabbage, very finely
  shredded

¾ tsp fine salt

150g (5oz/½ cup) small cooked,
  peeled prawns (defrosted if frozen),
  chopped into small pieces

2–3 tsp grated fresh root ginger,
  (around 2–3cm/¾–1¼in piece)

2 garlic cloves, crushed

½ mild red chilli, deseeded and finely
  chopped

1 spring onion, very finely chopped

1 tsp cornflour

1 tsp sesame oil

½ tsp sugar

1 tsp sake (or use dry sherry instead)

2 tsp soy sauce

❋ FOR THE DIPPING SAUCE

2 tbsp light soy sauce

½ tsp rice wine vinegar

½ tsp chilli oil

❋ FOR THE CABBAGE SALAD

¼ tsp sea salt

½ tsp caster sugar

1 tsp rice wine vinegar

½ tsp sesame oil

½ tsp light soy sauce

1 small garlic clove, sliced very thinly

200g (7oz/1⅔ cups) Chinese, spring
  or Napa cabbage, finely shredded

chilli flakes, to taste

This may look like a long list of ingredients, but you probably have most of them in your storecupboard. Choose the small Atlantic prawns, which have a lovely sweet taste and are easy to chop into small pieces, which is essential for this recipe. They're available both in the chilled section and freezer section in supermarkets or fishmongers.

Mix all the dipping sauce ingredients together in a small bowl. Set aside.

For the cabbage salad, put the salt, sugar, vinegar, sesame oil, soy sauce and garlic into a large bowl. Add the cabbage and a pinch of the chilli flakes and mix well. Set aside.

Next, prepare the filling. Put the cabbage into a bowl and sprinkle over the salt. Rub the salt in to give the cabbage a bit of a massage. Leave for 10–15 minutes, then drain well and squeeze to remove any moisture.

Place the prawns in a separate large bowl with the ginger, garlic, chilli and spring onion. Add the cabbage to the bowl. Sprinkle over the cornflour, then pour in the sesame oil, sugar, sake and soy sauce and mix everything together.

Lay out the wrappers, a few at a time, on a board. Fill a small bowl with cold water. Place a good heaped teaspoon of the filling in the centre of each wrapper, then dip your finger in the water and run it around the edge. Pinch the nearest side of the wrapper together, then use your two thumbs to work together and pleat the front of the wrapper five, six or seven times, squeezing it against the back of the wrapper as you move along. The back should be smooth and the front pleated so you end up with the classic dumpling shape. Place on a plate or tray and continue filling and wrapping until you've made them all.

Cook the dumplings in two batches. Heat 1–2 teaspoons sunflower or vegetable oil in a large frying pan over a medium heat. Fry the dumplings, flat-side down, for about 2 minutes until a golden crust forms on the bottom. Add 75ml (2½fl oz/⅓ cup) water and immediately cover. Reduce the heat to low-medium and let the steam cook the dumplings for 8 minutes or until all the water has evaporated. Remove the lid and let the dumplings cook for a further minute until they lift off from the bottom of the pan. You might need a spatula to help them along if they are a little sticky, but be careful not to break the wrappers. Repeat with the second batch.

Serve the hot dumplings with the cabbage salad and dipping sauce.

ほうれん草が入った 餃子の皮   *SPINACH GYOZA WRAPPERS*

Makes
34

60g (2¼oz/2 cups) spinach
½ tsp salt
160g (5½oz/1½ cups) plain flour, plus
   a little extra to knead
cornflour, to dust

A big handful of spinach will transform the simple gyoza dough into a cool-looking green wrapper. Instead of water, spinach purée is kneaded into the flour and the dough is used to make the wrappers for the Tofu and Spinach Gyoza (see page 106; also tip below).

Put the spinach into a small blender with the salt and 2 tablespoons water. Blend, scraping the mixture down every now and then, to make a smooth purée.

Sift the flour into a bowl and make a well in the middle. Add the spinach purée and 2 tablespoons water and stir together.

Keep stirring until the mixture looks crumbly, then bring it together with your hands and roughly knead in the bowl to mop up all the excess bits.

Put the dough onto a clean work surface or board and knead for 10 minutes until smooth and no cracks appear in the dough. If the dough feels sticky, continue to add a little more flour, 1 teaspoon at a time, until it has the right consistency.

Divide the dough into two even pieces and roll out until each measures around 17cm (6½in). Wrap in clingfilm or put in a sealable bag and leave to rest for 30 minutes at room temperature.

When you're ready to roll, fill a small pot with cornflour so you can dip into it as you need to while rolling out.

Dust a clean work surface or board and a rolling pin with cornflour.

Slice the first roll into 17 even-sized pieces. Each will weigh around 8g (¼oz). Take one piece and, keeping the other pieces covered, roll the piece out into a circle until it measures around 8cm (3¼in) in diameter. Put on a plate.

Continue with all the pieces, then repeat with the other log to make 34 wrappers in total.

Keep the wrappers covered as they're quite delicate and can dry out quickly.

TIP

This recipe would also work well for the classic pork filling and the prawn filling, too. Just make around double the filling mixture so you'll have enough. Any leftovers can be rolled into balls, fried off and used to toss with noodles or to add to miso or chicken soup.

豆腐とほうれん草の餃子

TOFU AND SPINACH GYOZA

Makes
34

20 spinach dumpling wrappers (see page 105)

✳ FOR THE FILLING

300g (10½oz/1⅔ cups) block firm tofu, drained well

1 fat garlic clove, crushed

1 heaped tbsp ginger purée (around 2cm/¾in piece, peeled and grated)

¾ tbsp tamari soy sauce, plus extra to serve

½ tbsp sesame oil

1 tbsp shaoxing rice wine

½ tsp salt

½ tsp freshly ground black pepper

1–2 tbsp sunflower or vegetable oil, plus extra for frying

125g (4½oz/4 cups) spinach, chopped

25g (1oz/½ cup) coriander, finely chopped

2 tsp cornflour

1 nori half sheet, cut into very thin strips, to garnish

✳ TO SERVE

Soy sauce

These eye-catching green dumplings are actually pretty easy to put together. They can also be made up to two days before if you want to get ahead. Just store in an airtight container in the fridge.

Put the tofu into a food processor and whizz to finely chop it. It should look very crumbly.

Tip into a large bowl. Add the garlic, ginger, soy sauce, sesame oil, rice wine, salt and pepper. Mix everything together well.

Heat a large frying pan and add the oil. Once the oil is hot, add the tofu mixture and cook for 10 minutes, stirring every now and then until the mixture starts to turn golden. Add the spinach and coriander and cook for 1–2 minutes more.

Take the pan off the heat, tip the mixture into a heatproof bowl and cool. Once cool, check the seasoning, then stir in the cornflour.

Fill a small bowl with cold water. Rest a wrapper between the thumb and forefinger of one hand. Use a teaspoon to place around 1½–2 teaspoons of the mixture into the middle, leaving a border of around 1cm (½in). Dip a finger into the water, then run it around the edge of the wrapper. Fold the wrapper in half to make a crescent shape.

Pinch the edge on one side of the wrapper to start to seal it. With your forefinger supporting the back of the wrapper, use your two thumbs to pleat the front of the wrapper. As you move along and start to shape the gyoza from one side to the other, keep pressing the front and back together with the forefinger and thumb of your hand. You'll end up with a curve of seven or eight pleats on the front of the gyoza and a smooth edge on the back. Fill all the wrappers in this way.

Cook the dumplings in two batches. Heat a little extra sunflower or vegetable oil in a large frying pan over a medium heat. Fry the dumplings, flat-side down, for about 2 minutes until a golden crust forms on the bottom. Add 75ml (2½ fl oz/⅓ cup) water, immediately cover with a lid, and let the steam cook the dumplings for 8 minutes or until all the water has evaporated.

Remove the lid and let the dumplings cook for a further minute until they lift off from the bottom of the pan easily. You might need a spatula to help them along if they are a little sticky, being careful not to break the wrapper. Remove to a plate and keep hot. Repeat with the second batch.

Sprinkle the nori strips over the gyoza and serve hot with a little pot of soy sauce to dip into.

See photograph overleaf.

TIP

Gyoza can be shaped in lots of different ways. For the alternative shape, shown in photograph overleaf, take the wrapper and spoon in the filling, shaping it into a sausage shape. Holding the wrapper in one hand, pull the top end of the wrapper up and over the filling and start to pinch the pastry alternately together. Once you've done this three or four times, fold it over the filling, then continue to do this, pinching and pulling down alternately until you reach the end of the filling. Once it's all enclosed, twirl the dough together at the end to create a teardrop shape.

焼きアスパラガスの 胡麻和え

SESAME-GRILLED ASPARAGUS RAFTS

16–24 thick asparagus spears

2 tbsp sesame oil

1 tbsp soy sauce

1 garlic clove, crushed

2 tbsp mix of black and white sesame
seeds

sea salt and freshly ground black
pepper

You'll also need 8–12 thin skewers –
use either bamboo (see tip on page
120) or metal.

**These cute-looking asparagus rafts are easy to do and, because they're
cooked quite quickly, the vegetables remain lovely and tender.**

Holding an asparagus spear in one hand, use the other hand to grab the base and
bend the stalk until it snaps – this gets rid of the woody stalk. Do the same with
all the other asparagus spears.

Place 4 asparagus spears next to one another. Skewer them crossways in two or
three places – just below the tips and 3cm (1¼in) from the bottom – with slender
bamboo or metal skewers. You will end up with something that looks like a raft.

Pour the sesame oil into a small bowl, then add the soy sauce, garlic and sesame
seeds and stir together to mix. Brush on both sides of the asparagus rafts. Season
the asparagus with a pinch of salt and lots of black pepper.

Preheat the grill until hot. Lay the spears on a lipped baking sheet and grill for
4–5 minutes on each side, using tongs to turn over halfway through. Serve hot.

焼き豆腐のピリ辛 ピーナッツソース和え

GRILLED TOFU SKEWERS WITH SPICY PEANUT SAUCE

❋ FOR THE TOFU SKEWERS

350g (12oz/2 cups) extra-firm
    tofu, drained and pressed for
    30 minutes or longer (see tip on
    page 70)
2 tbsp soy sauce
1 tbsp maple or agave syrup
½ tsp smoked paprika
½ tsp garlic powder

❋ FOR THE SPICY PEANUT SAUCE

100g (3½oz/generous ⅜ cup) smooth
peanut butter
4 tbsp coconut milk (see tip, below)
2 tbsp soy sauce
2 tbsp lime juice (around ½ juicy lime)
1 tbsp Sriracha or similar hot
    sauce (or to taste)
¼ tsp garlic powder

❋ TO SERVE

1 lime, cut into 4 or 6 wedges
handful of coriander, roughly
    chopped
1 tablespoon roasted
    peanuts, roughly chopped

You'll also need 8 skewers – use
    either bamboo (see tip on page
    120) or metal.

There's a big kick of spice here from the smoked paprika and garlic powder and, combined with the coconut-peanut sauce, makes these tofu skewers particularly addictive. It's the perfect vegan supper, alongside a bowl of rice or noodles and some stir-fried vegetables. If you want to turn them into a starter, cut the tofu pieces in half to make 16 small skewers.

Cut the pressed tofu block into 8 long sticks. Add the soy sauce, 2 tablespoons water, maple or agave syrup, smoked paprika and garlic powder to a sealable bag or dish and mix. Add the tofu to the mixture, turn to coat and leave to marinate, covered, in the fridge for a minimum of 30 minutes or up to 3 days.

Make the spicy peanut sauce. Put all the ingredients together in a small bowl and stir everything together (see tip below).

When you're ready to grill the tofu, thread the tofu lengthways onto the skewers. Heat your barbecue or griddle pan over a medium-high heat. When hot, grill the skewers for 10–15 minutes, turning as needed until grill marks form on each side, brushing with the leftover marinade as they cook. Remove from the heat and serve with the lime, coriander and nuts. Serve hot with the spicy peanut sauce on the side for dipping.

> **TIP**
> Both the marinade and the sauce can be made ahead. They'll keep in the fridge for up to 3 days. If the peanut sauce is a little thick, add 1–2 tablespoons cold water and stir in to loosen the mixture. The sauce is also better when it has been left for a while so that the ingredients have had time to meld together.

焼き鳥

YAKITORI CHICKEN SKEWERS

Serves
4–6

125ml (4fl oz/½ cup) soy sauce

2 tablespoons mirin

2 tablespoons rice wine vinegar

100g (3½oz/½ cup) light brown sugar

1 tsp fresh minced root ginger

1 garlic clove, crushed

5 tsp cornflour

800g (1¾lb) skinless, boneless
  chicken thighs, cut into pieces
  around 2.5 x 3cm (1–1¼in)

2 tbsp vegetable oil

1 tsp sesame seeds

sea salt and freshly ground black
  pepper

You'll also need 8 skewers – use
  either bamboo (see tip on page
  120) or metal.

The marinade for this recipe is used to keep the chicken tender, but also doubles up to become a sauce to drizzle over the top once the meat is cooked. Light brown soft sugar is used here to sweeten, but you can also use honey, but don't use one that's too floral or it will overpower the taste of the other ingredients.

Put the soy sauce into a medium saucepan and add the mirin, vinegar, sugar, ginger, garlic and cornflour. Pour in 75ml (2½fl oz/⅓ cup) water and place the pan over a medium heat. Whisk everything together until smooth and the cornflour dissolves into the mixture. Once the mixture is boiling, simmer for 1 minute until the mixture thickens. Pour half of it into a heatproof bowl and set aside.

Thread the chicken pieces onto skewers. Season all over with salt and pepper. Drizzle the skewers with the oil to prevent the chicken from sticking when cooking.

Preheat the grill to high. Lay the chicken skewers on a lipped baking tray. Brush the chicken with a little sauce from the saucepan and grill the chicken for 4 minutes. Flip over and baste the cooked side with the sauce. Cook for a further 4 minutes.

Flip the skewers over again and baste with more sauce. Cook for a further 4 minutes. Flip the skewers over again, baste and cook for another 4 minutes until the chicken is cooked through.

Sprinkle the skewers with the sesame seeds. Serve immediately with the reserved sauce.

TIP
If you need to skin and bone the chicken thighs, you'll need to buy 1.2kg (2¾lb) chicken thighs (with skin and bone) to yield the correct weight here.

牛焼き

GYU YAKI –
JAPANESE BEEF SKEWERS

Serves
4–6

25g (1oz/⅛ cup) caster sugar

3 tbsp soy sauce

1 tbsp sake

1 small piece fresh root ginger,
grated (about 1 tsp)

1–2 garlic cloves, crushed

1 tbsp sesame seeds (add more to
taste)

1½ tbsp sunflower or vegetable oil

2 spring onions, chopped

500g (18oz) beef flank steak, thinly
sliced into small pieces, each
around 2 x 5cm (¾ x 2in)

You'll also need 8 skewers – use
either bamboo (see tip below) or
metal.

These skewers of juicy morsels of steak (*gyu* in Japanese) are marinated
in soy sauce and sake to tenderise with ginger, garlic and spring onions.
Although they can be cooked as soon as they're mixed with the
marinade, they're better when it's had time to work its magic. Don't
leave it for too long though or the soy sauce will penetrate the meat and
make it too salty – between 2–4 hours is best.

If you want to cook these on the barbecue, wait until the coals are
covered in white ash before putting the skewers on top of the grill.

Put the sugar, soy sauce, sake, ginger, garlic, sesame seeds, oil and spring onions
in a resealable food bag or large sealable container. Add the beef and stir all the
ingredients together until the pieces of meat are completely coated. Cover and
leave to marinate in the fridge for 2–4 hours.

Take each skewer and push several pieces of beef onto it. Spoon any spare bits
of spring onion and the little bit of marinade that's left over in the bowl onto
the beef. There shouldn't be much left and there's no need to brush additional
marinade on the meat while it's cooking.

When you're ready to cook the skewers, preheat the grill until hot.

Grill the beef (or cook on the barbecue) until the beef is done to your liking –
about 3 minutes on each side is good. Because the meat is thinly sliced, you'll
find that it cooks fairly quickly. Be careful not to overcook or burn the meat or the
texture will become tough.

TIP
If you're using bamboo skewers,
soak them in a bowl of water
for 30 minutes beforehand so
that they don't burn.

チキンラーメン **ORIGINAL RAMEN**

❀ FOR THE RAMEN

20g (¾oz) dried black fungus
    mushrooms
200g (7oz) dried buckwheat noodles
    (or see tip on page 129 for soba
    noodles)
1.4 litres (2½ pints) soup base (see
    Soup recipe on page 126)
2 medium eggs
4 tsp tonkatsu paste
2 tbsp Mayu garlic oil (see tip on
    page 123)
200g (7oz/4 cups) beansprouts
20–30g (¾–1¼oz) kizami red ginger
    (or sushi ginger)
2 spring onions, finely sliced
sesame seeds, to sprinkle
½ seaweed sheet, shredded

❀ FOR THE CHASHU CHICKEN

4 boneless chicken thighs
2 tsp vegetable or sunflower oil
4 tbsp soy sauce
4 tbsp shaoxing rice wine
2 tbsp caster sugar
sea salt and freshly ground black
    pepper

You'll also need cooking string.

The chicken needs to be made ahead here so it can marinate in the rich, salty, sweet sauce, but it's very easy to do. It's well worth the work as this method of cooking gives the meat a wonderful umami flavour. If there's any leftover stock from cooking the chicken (although very salty), it can be used to lightly dress noodles mixed with steamed vegetables.

Make the chashu chicken. Put the chicken on a board, season all over and roll each piece up. Wrap some string around it two or three times to secure. Heat the oil in a medium frying pan over a medium-high heat and pan-fry the chicken until golden all over, turning occasionally, for around 4–5 minutes in total. It doesn't need to be cooked all the way through. Set aside on a plate.

Pour the soy sauce, wine and sugar into a small pan (the chicken needs to fit snugly on the base with not too much space around it), then pour in 250ml (9fl oz/generous 1 cup) cold water. When the chicken is in the pan, the liquid should rise halfway up the side of it. Heat to dissolve the sugar, then add the chicken and any of its juices and bring to a simmer. Cover the pan with a lid and simmer for 15–20 minutes, turning halfway through. Transfer to a heatproof bowl with the liquid. Cool, then transfer to the fridge to chill for at least 3 hours or overnight.

When you're ready to make the ramen, put the black fungus mushrooms in a bowl of hot water and set aside to rehydrate. Cook the noodles according to the packet instructions, then drain in a colander and cool under cold running water.

Pour the soup base into a large pan and bring to a simmer. Meanwhile, cook the eggs. Carefully lower the eggs into a saucepan of boiling water, reduce the heat a little and simmer for 7 minutes. Transfer to a bowl of iced water and leave for 4–5 minutes. Lift out and set aside.

Add the tonkatsu paste to the soup base, along with the garlic oil and whisk in. Add the noodles to the pan. Add most of the beansprouts to the pan, leaving a handful for the garnish.

Slice the chicken on a board (discarding the string). Peel the eggs and drain the black mushrooms. Divide the noodles and beansprouts among four bowls and ladle in the soup. Top each with an equal portion of chicken. Next, divide the black mushrooms, reserved bean sprouts, ginger, spring onions, sesame seeds and the seaweed among the bowls. Halve the eggs and place on top, then serve.

野菜ラーメン　　　*VEGETABLE RAMEN*

Serves
4

❋ FOR THE VEGETABLE SOUP BASE

1.4 litres (2½ pints) cold water
2 vegetable stock cubes, crumbled
2½ tbsp soy sauce
15g (½oz) dashi powder
1 dried shiitake mushroom
salt and freshly ground black pepper

❋ FOR THE RAMEN

20g (¾oz) dried black fungus
　mushrooms
200g (7oz) dried buckwheat noodles
2 medium eggs
200g (7oz/2⅔ cups) savoy or
　Chinese cabbage, finely shredded
150g (5oz/3 cups) carrots, cut into
　thin batons
200g (7oz/4 cups) beansprouts
2 spring onions, finely sliced
20–30g (¾–1¼oz) kizami red ginger
　(or sushi ginger)
½ seaweed sheet, shredded
sesame seeds, to sprinkle
2 tbsp Mayu garlic oil (see tip below)

> **TIP**
> To make garlic oil, put 2 tablespoons sunflower or vegetable oil into a small frying pan and add 2 smashed garlic cloves. Heat over a low heat for around 2 minutes to infuse the oil with the garlic. Discard the garlic and use the oil to drizzle over the ramen.

This bowl of broth is full-to-the-brim with goodness as it's packed with lots of vegetables and filling noodles. It's topped with half a boiled egg, but to make it vegan, serve with a slice of pan-fried firm tofu instead.

Start by making the soup base. Put all the ingredients into a large saucepan, season with the salt and pepper, and bring to the boil. Reduce the heat to a simmer and cook for 10 minutes. Lift out the shiitake mushroom and discard. If you want to make the stock as clear as possible, strain it into a clean pan once it has finished simmering.

While the soup is simmering, put the black fungus mushrooms in a bowl of hot water and set aside. Cook the noodles according to the packet instructions, then drain in a colander and cool under cold running water.

Meanwhile, carefully lower the eggs into a saucepan of boiling water, reduce the heat a little and simmer for 7 minutes. Transfer to a bowl of iced water and leave for 4–5 minutes. Lift out and set aside.

Once the soup base is ready, keep the heat at a low simmer. Drain the rehydrated black fungus mushrooms. Add them to the soup base with the cabbage and carrots and simmer for 5 minutes. After 4 minutes, add most of the beansprouts (reserving a few for garnish) for the last minute of the cooking time.

While the vegetables are simmering, peel the eggs. Keep them on a board or plate until you're ready to use them.

Divide the noodles, then the vegetables (lift these from the soup base with a slotted spoon) among four bowls. Ladle the soup base into the bowls, too. Garnish with the remaining beansprouts, the spring onions, the ginger and the shredded seaweed. Sprinkle over a few sesame seeds and drizzle over the garlic oil. Cut the eggs in half and place half on each bowl.

チキンラーメン
CHICKEN RAMEN

❀ FOR THE RAMEN

1 x quantity Chicken Chashu (see page 122), chilled

2 medium eggs

10g (¼oz) dried black fungus mushrooms

200g (7oz) dried buckwheat noodles (or see tip on page 129 for soba noodles)

1–2 tbsp Mayu garlic oil, or to taste (or see tip on page 123)

200g (7oz/4 cups) beansprouts

125g (4½oz/1⅔ cups) iceberg lettuce, shredded

1 carrot, shredded or coarsely grated

❀ FOR THE CHICKEN STOCK

2 chicken carcasses

6 black peppercorns

1 medium carrot

1 garlic clove, smashed

½ leek

1 small onion, halved

The base of this ramen comes from making a simple chicken stock – just simmer the bones of the chicken and some vegetables in water to garner the goodness. You can make the chicken stock up to four days ahead if you need to and keep it stored in the fridge. It freezes well, too, for up to three months.

Start by making the chicken stock. Put the chicken carcasses into a large pan. Add the peppercorns, carrot, garlic, leek and onion. Pour over 2 litres (3½ pints) cold water, then cover the pan with a lid. Bring to the boil and, as soon as the liquid is boiling, reduce the heat to the lowest setting and cook on a very low simmer for 1 hour. Strain into a clean pan – there should be around 1.4 litres (2½ pints) stock. Add a splash more water if it needs topping up.

When you're ready to make the ramen, take the chicken chashu out of the fridge to come up to room temperature.

Next, cook the eggs. Carefully lower the eggs into a saucepan of boiling water, reduce the heat a little and simmer for 7 minutes. Lift into a bowl of iced water and leave for 4–5 minutes. Remove and peel off the shells. Set aside.

While the eggs are boiling, put the dried black fungus mushrooms in a bowl of hot water and set aside to rehydrate.

Cook the noodles in a pan of boiling water, according to the instructions on the pack. Drain in a colander and cool under cold running water.

Put the chicken on a board, discarding the string, and slice into finger-width strips.

Pour the stock into a large pan and stir in the garlic oil. Add the noodles and the beansprouts, reserving a handful to garnish.

Divide this evenly among four large soup bowls. Divide up the chicken, black mushrooms, reserved beansprouts, lettuce and carrot equally and put on top of each bowl. Finally, slice the eggs in half and put a half on each bowl, then serve.

牛肉ラーメン

BEEF RAMEN

✿ FOR THE RAMEN

10g (¼oz) dried black fungus
  mushrooms
2 medium eggs
1–2 tsp sunflower or vegetable oil
2 x 250g (9oz) sirloin steaks
200g (7oz) dried buckwheat
  noodles (or see tip on page 129 for
  soba noodles)
200g (7oz/2 cups) beansprouts
125g (4½oz/1 cup) baby corn, sliced
20g (¾oz) kizami red ginger (or sushi
  ginger)
2 spring onions, finely sliced
½ seaweed sheet, shredded
1 medium red chilli, thinly sliced
sea salt and freshly ground black
  pepper

✿ FOR THE SOUP

1.4 litres (2½ pints) vegetable soup
  base (see page 123) or
chicken stock (see page 124)
40–60g (1¼–2½oz) tonkatsu paste
1–2 tbsp Mayu garlic oil, or to taste
  (see tip on page 123)

**Pan-frying the steak in a hot pan to brown before slicing into strips gives
more flavour to this recipe and leaves the pieces really tender, too.**

Soak the black fungus mushrooms in a bowl of hot water. Set aside.

Next, cook the eggs. Carefully lower the eggs into a pan of boiling water, reduce
the heat a little and simmer for 7 minutes. Lift into a bowl of iced water and leave
for 4–5 minutes. Remove and peel off the shells. Set aside.

Heat the oil in a large frying pan. Season the steaks all over and as soon as the oil
has heated through, add the steaks to the pan. Cook for around 2–3 minutes on
each side for medium–rare to medium or until they're done to how you like them.
Set aside to rest.

Cook the noodles in a pan of boiling water, according to the instructions on the
pack. Drain in a colander and cool under cold running water.

Pour the soup base into a large pan and add the tonkatsu paste. Place over a
medium heat and bring to the boil, whisking well to dissolve the paste. Add the
garlic oil to taste.

Add the cooked noodles, the beansprouts (reserving a handful to garnish), the
baby corn and black mushrooms. Divide evenly among four large soup bowls.

Slice the steaks into finger-width strips and put on top. Garnish with the reserved
beansprouts, ginger, spring onions and seaweed. Slice each egg in half and place
a half on top of each bowl, then sprinkle over a few slices of chillies and serve.

辛口味噌ラーメン　　*SPICY MISO RAMEN*

❀ FOR THE RAMEN

2 medium eggs

5–8g (⅛–¼oz) dried black fungus
　mushrooms

200g (7oz) dried buckwheat noodles
　(or see tip below for soba noodles)

200g (7oz/4 cups) beansprouts

10–15g (¼–½oz) kizami red ginger
　(or sushi ginger)

1 medium red chilli, finely sliced

2 spring onions, finely sliced

½ seaweed sheet, shredded

sesame seeds, to sprinkle

❀ FOR THE CHASHU PORK

2 x 250g (9oz) pork shoulder steaks

1 tsp sunflower or vegetable oil

4 tbsp soy sauce

4 tbsp shaoxing rice wine

2 tbsp caster sugar

salt and freshly ground black pepper

❀ FOR THE SPICY MISO SOUP

1.4 litres (2½ pints) good-quality
　vegetable or chicken stock (or see
　recipe for the vegetable soup base,
　page 123 or chicken stock on
　page 124)

4 pinches cayenne pepper, or to taste

40–60g (1½oz–2¼oz) tonkatsu paste

80g (3oz) Japanese miso dare (use
　white miso for a light flavour or red
　for a fuller flavour)

chilli oil, to season

The cayenne pepper provides a pleasing touch of spice in this ramen. When you're using it to season the base, add it pinch by pinch – too much will spoil the stock and unbalance the flavour. The chashu pork needs to be made ahead so it has time to marinate before you make the ramen, but it will sit in the fridge for up to three days if you need it to.

Prepare the chashu pork. Put the pork on a board and season each steak all over. Heat the oil in a medium frying pan and brown the pork for around 2 minutes on each side until golden. Set the pan aside.

Pour 250ml (9fl oz/generous 1 cup) water into a medium saucepan, then add the soy sauce, wine and caster sugar. Heat gently to dissolve the sugar, then add the browned pork steaks to the pan. Cover the pan with a lid and bring the liquid to a simmer. Reduce the heat to its lowest setting and simmer the pork for around 1 hour, turning the pieces over halfway through. The liquid will reduce and become thicker over this time and the pork will become more tender.

Lift the pork into a sealable, heatproof container and pour over the remaining liquid. Cool, then transfer to the fridge for 3 hours or overnight. If you're making the stock for the spicy miso soup from scratch, make this now and pour into an airtight container and cool and chill.

When you're ready to make the ramen, bring a pan of water to the boil. Carefully lower in the eggs, reduce the heat a little and simmer for 7 minutes. Lift into a bowl of iced water and leave for 4–5 minutes, then remove and peel the eggs. Set aside.

While the eggs are boiling, put the dried black fungus mushrooms in a bowl of hot water and set aside to rehydrate.

Cook the noodles in a pan of boiling water, according to the instructions on the pack. Drain and cool under cold running water.

Take the pork out of the fridge and lift out of the marinade. Slice into finger-width strips.

Pour the stock for the soup into a large pan and add the cayenne pepper. Place the pan over a medium heat and bring to a simmer. Put the tonkatsu paste and miso into a bowl, mix together, then whisk into the stock. Add the chilli oil, to season.

Add the cooked noodles to the stock, followed by the beansprouts (leaving a handful aside to garnish). Divide among four large soup bowls.

Add an equal portion of pork, black mushrooms, ginger and sliced chilli. Next, add the spring onions, seaweed and a sprinkling of sesame seeds. Finally, slice the eggs in half and put a half on top of each bowl, then serve, garnished with those reserved beansprouts.

TIP

If you buy soba noodles, which are a variation of buckwheat noodles, you won't need to cook as many. Use two 80g (3oz) bundles of dried soba noodles for four servings.

CHAPTER 6

✳

TEMPURA

満腹

manpuku

—

A full stomach.

You will probably need no encouragement, but these light, crisp morsels, one of the cornerstones of Japanese cooking, must be eaten as soon as they are cooked. They are believed to have been around since the late sixteenth century – it's thought the principle was introduced by Portuguese Catholic missionaries and other workers who would make fritters before they had to fast. Lard would probably have been used then, but it's thought that the basic batter recipe would have been much the same.

It's super simple to make – just iced water, flour, egg and salt – but treat it lightly just as the Japanese do and whisk everything just until all the ingredients come together. Otherwise, you'll find the cooked batter at the end will be tough. In fact, the traditional way to mix the batter is with chopsticks, as the tapered ends cut lightly through the liquid to mix it into the dry flour. A few lumps are absolutely fine in there.

When preparing the ingredients, try to keep them all about the same size so they cook in around the same amount of time. The principles of deep-frying are the same here as with other deep-fried food: maintain the temperature of the oil by testing regularly (a metal-stemmed thermometer is useful if you're not using a deep-fat fryer) and don't overcrowd the pan so that the temperature doesn't reduce.

Drop the pieces onto kitchen paper as soon as they're whipped out of the hot oil to soak up any excess and sprinkle with a little salt, to help cut through the greasiness. They're at their best still hot, having had a few seconds to cool down so the batter is still crisp, so have the dipping sauce ready and gather everyone round so you can serve them in batches as soon as they're cooked.

エビ天麩羅ネギ和え   PRAWN TEMPURA WITH SPRING ONIONS

sunflower oil or vegetable oil, for frying

a cube of bread, for testing the oil, if needed

150g (5oz/1⅓ cups) plain flour

1 large egg

200ml (7fl oz/scant 1 cup) cold water

handful of ice cubes, to chill the water

500g (18oz) raw, peeled king prawns, leaving the tails on if you can, patted dry with kitchen paper

2 spring onions, finely sliced

salt

soy sauce, to serve

Dipping prawns in a light tempura batter, then cooking in a pot of hot oil leaves them wonderfully tender. The temperature of the oil will drop after cooking, so check it once you've lifted a batch out. If you're not going to eat the hot prawns immediately, keep them warm in a low oven. There's plenty of batter for the prawns so if you have any vegetables you want to use up, chop them into strips and dip into the leftover batter and drop in and cook until crisp. See our recipe on page 135.

Heat the oil in a deep-fat fryer or wok to 180°C/350°F or until a cube of bread dropped into the oil sizzles and turns a light golden in around 20–30 seconds. Line a large tray with kitchen paper.

Sift the flour into a bowl. Add a pinch of salt. Set aside.

Crack the egg into a separate bowl and gently whisk until the yolk and the white are just combined. If you have any chopsticks to hand, use them as it's the traditional way to do this part of the recipe.

Put the water and ice cubes into a bowl and swirl the ice around to chill the water quickly. Strain 200ml (7fl oz/scant 1 cup) of the chilled water into a measuring jug, then pour into the bowl containing the beaten egg.

Add the flour into the bowl and lightly whisk together, but be careful not to overmix the batter – a few lumps is fine.

Lower the prawns into the batter and lift them out with a slotted spoon to drain away any excess batter. Carefully lower them, a few at a time, into the hot oil and deep-fry in batches until crisp and a pale golden colour, about 2 minutes.

Using a clean slotted spoon, lift the prawns onto the kitchen paper to drain and then onto a large serving plate. Sprinkle with salt and serve with the spring onions sprinkled over the top and soy sauce to dip into.

VEGETABLE TEMPURA WITH TOASTED SESAME SEEDS

Serves
4

sunflower oil or vegetable oil, for frying

a cube of bread, for testing the oil,
   if needed

150g (5oz/1⅓ cups) plain flour

1 large egg

200ml (7fl oz/scant 1 cup) cold water

handful of ice cubes, to chill the water

2 tsp toasted sesame seeds, plus
   extra to garnish

500g (18oz) prepared vegetables,
   such as red onion, green beans,
   aubergine, courgette, red pepper,
   broccoli, sweet potato, carrot
   (see tip)

salt

soy sauce, to serve

A variety of colourful vegetables and shapes will keep the finished selection looking really interesting. The batter doesn't need to sit and rest before using, so prep the vegetables first before mixing it up. For a vegan batter, use the batter recipe for the tofu tempura on page 138. The pieces are best fresh from the pan, but if you want to keep them warm, put into a low oven.

Heat the oil in a deep-fat fryer or wok to 190°C/375°F or until a cube of bread dropped into the oil sizzles and turns a light golden in around 20–30 seconds. Line a large tray with kitchen paper.

Sift the flour into a bowl. Add a pinch of salt. Set aside.

Crack the egg into a separate bowl and gently whisk until the yolk and the white are just combined. If you have any chopsticks to hand, use them as it's the traditional way to do this part of the recipe.

Put the water and ice cubes into a bowl and swirl the ice around to chill the water quickly. Strain 200ml (7fl oz/scant 1 cup) of the chilled water into a measuring jug, then pour into the bowl containing the beaten egg.

Add the flour and the sesame seeds into the bowl and lightly whisk together, but be careful not to overmix the batter – a few lumps is fine.

Lower the vegetables into the batter and lift them out with a slotted spoon to drain away any excess batter. Carefully lower them, a few at a time, into the hot oil and deep-fry in batches until crisp and a pale golden colour, about 3–4 minutes.

Using a clean slotted spoon, lift the vegetables onto the kitchen paper to drain and then onto a large serving plate. Sprinkle with salt and a few extra sesame seeds and serve with soy sauce to dip into.

See photograph overleaf.

TIP

To ensure the vegetables cook evenly, chop each one into similar-size pieces. The green beans just need to have their stalks trimmed. For peppers, cut them in half, remove the stalk and seeds, then cut into 2cm/¾in thick pieces. For the courgette, chop into 1cm/½in thick rounds. For the red onion, pick a small-medium one and cut into 1cm/½in thick wedges. For broccoli, simply chop into even-sized florets. Sweet potatoes have a dense texture so need to be cut up smaller than these other pieces. Use a small piece and chop into slices, just less than 1cm/½in.

豆腐と唐辛子の
天麩羅

TOFU AND CHILLI TEMPURA

Serves
4

sunflower oil or vegetable oil, for
frying
a cube of bread, for testing the oil,
if needed
150g (5oz/1⅓ cups) plain flour
a couple of good pinches of chilli
flakes, depending on how much
spice you like, plus extra for
sprinkling
200ml (7fl oz/scant 1 cup) cold water
handful of ice cubes, to chill the
water
2 x 280g (10oz/1⅔ cups) firm tofu,
chopped into 2.5–3cm (1–1¼in)
cubes and drained on kitchen
paper
salt
soy sauce, to serve

This vegan recipe can be dressed up or down in terms of seasoning.
We've added a kick of heat from dried chilli flakes, but if you'd like to
add more flavour, try adding toasted sesame seeds and sliced spring
onions sprinkled over at the end, too. You need a firm tofu – not the
silken one – and depending on the variety it will need to be pressed (see
page 70) or drained to remove excess water from the block to keep the
tempura coating crisp. If you're not serving straightaway, keep batches
warm in a low oven.

Heat the oil in a deep-fat fryer or wok to 180°C/350°F or until a cube of bread
dropped into the oil sizzles and turns a light golden in around 20–30 seconds.
Line a large tray with kitchen paper.

Sift the flour into a bowl. Add a pinch of salt and some chilli flakes. Stir and set
aside.

Put the water and ice cubes into a bowl and swirl the ice around to chill the water
quickly. Strain 200ml (7fl oz/scant 1 cup) of the chilled water into a measuring jug,
then pour into the bowl of flour.

Whisk lightly, but be careful not to overmix the batter – a few lumps is fine.

Lower the tofu cubes into the batter and lift them out with a slotted spoon to drain
away any excess batter. Carefully lower them, a few at a time, into the hot oil and
deep-fry in batches until crisp and a pale golden colour, about 3–4 minutes.

Using a clean slotted spoon, lift the tofu cubes onto the kitchen paper to drain
and then onto a large serving plate. Sprinkle with salt and a few more chilli flakes
and serve with the soy sauce to dip into.

138   天ぷら   TEMPURA

ホタルイカ塩胡椒風味

SALT AND PEPPER BABY SQUID

sunflower oil or vegetable oil, for
  frying
a cube of bread, for testing the oil,
  if needed
75g (3oz/¾ cup) plain flour
½ large egg
100ml (3½fl oz/scant ½ cup) cold
  water
handful of ice cubes, to chill the
  water
400g (14oz) baby squid, cleaned
salt and freshly ground black pepper
soy sauce or sweet chilli sauce, to
  serve

Look for bags of baby squid, still with their tentacles attached, at your fishmonger or in the freezer section of your local supermarket. Squid needs to be cooked quickly to give it a lovely tender texture, so make sure the oil is up to temperature every time you lower a batch into the hot oil – it cools down considerably on cooking. This is seasoned with salt and black pepper and the more you add of the latter, the spicier the batter becomes. They really are best served hot from the pan.

Heat the oil in a deep-fat fryer or wok to 190°C/375°F or until a cube of bread dropped into the oil sizzles and turns a light golden in around 20–30 seconds. Line a large tray with kitchen paper.

Sift the flour into a bowl, then add ½ teaspoon salt and 10 twists of black pepper and set aside.

Crack the egg into a separate bowl and gently whisk until the yolk and the white are just combined. If you have any chopsticks to hand, use them as it's the traditional way to do this part of the recipe. Pour off half the beaten egg into a small bowl and chill so you can use it in another recipe.

Put the water and ice cubes into a bowl and swirl the ice around to chill the water quickly. Strain 100ml (3½fl oz/scant ½ cup) of the chilled water into the bowl containing the beaten egg.

Add the seasoned flour to the mixture. Whisk lightly together, but be careful not to overmix the batter – a few lumps is fine.

Lower 3 or 4 baby squid into the batter at a time and lift them out with a slotted spoon to drain away any excess batter. Carefully lower them into the hot oil and deep-fry in batches for 2–3 minutes until golden and crisp.

Using a clean slotted spoon, lift the baby squid onto the kitchen paper to drain and then onto a serving plate. Sprinkle with salt and serve with soy sauce or sweet chilli sauce to dip into.

軟殻蟹の天麩羅   *SOFT SHELL CRAB TEMPURA*

sunflower oil or vegetable oil,
  for frying
a cube of bread, for testing the oil,
  if needed
75g (3oz/¾ cup) plain flour
½ large egg
100ml (3½fl oz/scant ½ cup) cold
  water
handful of ice cubes, to chill the
  water
8 whole soft shell crabs, patted dry
  with kitchen paper
salt
soy sauce or sweet chilli sauce, to
  serve

You'll find soft shell crab in the freezer section of Asian supermarkets, sold in a box with each crab wrapped individually so you can take out as many as you need. There's plenty of meat on them and they're quite rich as you eat the whole thing including the shell. These are tossed in the simple tempura batter, but do add a pinch or two of chopped fresh chilli if you fancy a bit of heat. These are irresistible hot from the pan, but if you want to serve the whole batch together, lay them on a platter and keep warm in a low oven.

Heat the oil in a deep-fat fryer or wok to 190°C/375°F or until a cube of bread dropped into the oil sizzles and turns a light golden in around 20–30 seconds. Line a large tray with kitchen paper.

Sift the flour into a bowl. Add a pinch of salt. Set aside.

Crack the egg into a separate bowl and gently whisk until the yolk and the white are just combined. If you have any chopsticks to hand, use them as it's the traditional way to do this part of the recipe. Pour off half the beaten egg into a small bowl and chill so you can use it in another recipe.

Put the water and ice cubes into a bowl and swirl the ice around to chill the water quickly. Strain 100ml (3½fl oz/scant 1 cup) of the chilled water into a measuring jug, then pour into the bowl containing the beaten egg.

Add the seasoned flour into the bowl and lightly whisk together, but be careful not to overmix the batter – a few lumps is fine.

Lower a couple of crabs at a time into the batter and lift them out with a slotted spoon to drain away any excess batter. Carefully lower them into the hot oil and deep-fry in batches for 3–4 minutes until golden and crisp. They need to be quite crisp or the batter turns soggy on cooling.

Using a clean slotted spoon, lift the crabs onto the kitchen paper to drain, then onto a serving plate. Sprinkle with salt and serve with soy sauce or sweet chilli sauce to dip into.

TIP

For a quick spicy garnish, thinly slice 1 red chilli and 2 spring onions. Stir-fry in a pan with a little oil, seasoning as you do so, until golden. Spoon over the crabs just before serving.

CHAPTER 7

✳

DESSERTS

betsubara

別腹

—

'A different stomach' – being able to eat something sweet,
even though your stomach is full of savoury food.

The delicate flavours and textures of Japanese savoury recipes call for a simple sweet ending – think perfectly carved slices of fresh fruit and light-as-air sponges through to individual cheese tarts. One recipe is a simple riff on cheesecake featuring a sweetened homemade pastry. Refreshing ice cream with sumptuous texture and distinctive ingredients – matcha tea and Japanese sesame paste – also hits the spot.

Japanese cakes are made with a similar combination of ingredients to their western counterparts but the difference lies in the quantities. Butter is swapped for a small amount of light vegetable oil, for instance, and flour is used in a much lower quantity, too. But it's the eggs that hold the whole sponge together, which are whisked into the mix in different stages. The egg yolks are combined first with the sugar, then the flour and flavourings. But it's when the egg whites are whisked into clouds of white bubbles and just to that point when they hold soft peaks that the magic really happens. Once folded into the batter, they help to aerate the whole confection. This works beautifully in both the mini Green Tea Chiffon Cakes (see page 150) and the pretty Cherry Roll Cake (see page 146).

For biscuit-lovers, try the matcha cookies, studded with a pistachio. The melt-in-the-mouth texture is perfect with a cup of green tea at the end of a meal. They would also make an ideal gift. Pack them up in a minimalist box with a beautiful ribbon in true Japanese style, as the opening and sense of anticipation is almost as important as what's inside. If you're giving this to someone who's Japanese, don't be surprised if they give you a present in return, as thanking you for a gift by giving one in return is also a tradition. And, of course, this could go on and on…

チェリーロール *CHERRY ROLL CAKE*

Serves
6

❋ FOR THE SWISS ROLL

3 medium eggs, separated, and
  whites chilled
80g (3oz/generous ⅓ cup) granulated
  sugar
2 tbsp vegetable oil
1 tbsp cherry liqueur
pink or red natural food colouring
50g (2oz/½ cup) plain flour, sifted

❋ FOR THE FILLING AND TO DECORATE

200ml (7fl oz/scant 1 cup) double
  cream
20g (¾oz) granulated sugar
1 tbsp cherry liqueur
16 pitted cherries marinated in
  liqueur, plus more to serve, optional
icing sugar, for dusting

You'll also need a 23 x 33cm (9 x
  13in) Swiss roll tin.

If you're a fan of the classic Swiss roll, you'll love this twist which has a splash of cherry liqueur in the sponge and macerated cherries to finish. It's garnished with rosettes of cream, which also make it easy to slice into servings. Use the traditional Sakura cherry liqueur if you can get it or swap it with kirsch.

Preheat the oven to 210°C/410°F/gas mark 6½. Line the Swiss roll tin with baking parchment.

Start by making the Swiss roll. Put the egg yolks in a mixing bowl and whisk until smooth. Add 30g (1¼oz) of the sugar and whisk well until pale and thickened, around 1½–2 minutes. Continue to whisk and slowly add the vegetable oil, a little at a time, until the mixture looks thick and creamy.

In a small bowl, combine the liqueur, 4 teaspoons water and a little food colouring – use a few drops of liquid or a dab of paste, to give a pale pink colour. Pour into the egg mixture and whisk together to combine.

Add the flour and fold in with a spatula or large metal spoon. The mixture will now look like a thick-ish batter. Clean the beaters well.

In a separate large bowl, add the egg whites. Whisk until very lightly frothy, then slowly add the remaining sugar, a little at a time, whisking well until stiff peaks form and the meringue is thick and glossy.

Add a third of the meringue to the egg yolk mixture and whisk to combine. Add the rest of the meringue, in two halves, and fold in again using a spatula or large metal spoon.

Carefully pour the mixture into the lined tin and lightly spread it out so that it lies evenly. To knock out any air bubbles inside the mixture, lift the tray slightly off the work surface, then let it drop back down. Do this a couple of times.

Turn the oven down to 200°C/400°F/gas mark 6 and bake for 15 minutes.

Take the tin out of the oven and lift out the cake, still on the baking parchment, and transfer to a wire rack. Carefully lift the paper away from the edges of the cake to loosen.

Make the filling. Pour the cream into a bowl and add the sugar and cherry liqueur. Whip the cream until it forms thick but not stiff peaks. Put the bowl in the fridge until you're ready to use it.

When the cake is completely cold, spoon most of the cream mixture onto it, reserving a couple of spoonfuls for the decoration (put the remaining cream in the fridge). Spread the filling out with a knife, leaving a 2.5cm (1in) gap all the way around. Roughly chop 10 of the cherries and dot them over the cream.

Starting with a short end nearest you (and the lining paper still underneath), roll the cake carefully and tightly away from you, using the lining paper at the start to pick up the bottom edge, and leaving it behind as you continue to roll so it peels off the cake. When the cake is rolled up with the join underneath, wrap the roll in clingfilm.

Put on a plate and transfer to the fridge for at least 1 hour, or overnight.

When you're ready to serve, remove the clingfilm from the Swiss roll and put it on a board. Trim both ends off the cake for a neat finish. Pipe or spoon small blobs of the reserved cream and top each with a soaked cherry (drained first on kitchen paper). Dust lightly with icing sugar.

プリン

JAPANESE CUSTARD PUDDINGS

❋ FOR THE CARAMEL

125g (4½oz/½ cup) granulated sugar

❋ FOR THE PUDDINGS

3 medium eggs
2 medium egg yolks
60g (2¼oz/¼ cup) granulated sugar
½ tsp vanilla extract
550ml (19fl oz/2½ cups) whole milk
60ml (2¼fl oz/¼ cup) double cream

You will also need six 200ml (7fl oz/
   scant 1 cup) pudding moulds.

These are a delight. If you've never made caramel before, watch the bubbles carefully as it boils when it's turning golden. When the sound starts to subside, it's very nearly ready. Watch it carefully and whip it off the heat quickly before it turns dark golden and burns.

Preheat the oven to 150°C/300°F/gas mark 2. Place the pudding moulds in a deep roasting tin.

Make the caramel. Put the sugar in a small, heavy-based saucepan. Stir in 2 tablespoons water and place over a low–medium heat. Cook to dissolve the sugar, stirring occasionally to help all the grains of sugar dissolve.

When all the sugar has dissolved, turn up the heat to medium (there's no need to stir any more). As the syrup bubbles, cook until it starts to turn a very pale caramel colour. Shake or swirl the pan so that the syrup cooks evenly until it deepens and turns a deep golden amber colour. This will take around 10 minutes.

Take the pan off the heat and carefully and quickly pour the hot caramel between all the pudding moulds, making sure the caramel is spread evenly. Swirl each pot around as you fill them so that the caramel covers the bases. Take care – the syrup is very hot. Set aside.

To make the custard, put the eggs and egg yolks into a heatproof bowl and mix slowly with a wire whisk just until combined. Pour in the sugar and vanilla and mix gently until combined, again avoiding whisking in any air.

Pour the milk and cream into a saucepan and place over a medium heat. Stir with a wooden spoon until just boiling, then remove from the heat.

Pour around a quarter of the hot milk mix into your egg mixture and stir well using a spatula or a wooden spoon. Add the rest of the hot mix and stir together gently.

Strain this into a heatproof jug, then pour it equally among the moulds filled with the caramel sauce.

TIP

The secret to the super-smooth texture is to very lightly stir or whisk the ingredients together when first making the custard, as it's important not to introduce air bubbles into the mixture. The low temperature produces a wonderful silky texture at the end.

デザート

Pour enough hot water into the roasting tin around the moulds, until it comes halfway up the moulds. Bake for 25–35 minutes until softly set and the middles still have a slight wobble.

Remove from the oven and carefully lift the moulds out and onto a wire rack. Cool for 30 minutes, then refrigerate for at least 4–5 hours to set or ideally overnight.

To serve, run a knife around the top edge of each mould. Place a small plate (preferably with a slight edge to catch the caramel) face-down over the top of each pudding. Turn it over quickly and remove the mould. If the pudding doesn't release immediately, dip the mould in hot water for no more than 8–10 seconds.

抹茶の
シフォンケーキ

GREEN TEA CHIFFON CAKES

Makes
6

2 medium eggs, separated

50g (2oz/¼ cup) granulated sugar

2 tbsp vegetable oil

2 tbsp cold water

60g (2¼oz/½ cup) plain flour

1 tsp baking powder

4 tsp matcha powder, plus extra to
   dust

icing sugar, to dust, optional

❀ TO SERVE

1 mango, peeled, stoned and finely
   sliced

You'll also need a 6-hole muffin tray,
   lined with paper cases.

It's the combination of oil and water that produces these muffin-sized light-textured sponges. Serve with finely sliced mango and, if you like, a small scoop of vanilla ice cream. Finish with a dusting of matcha and icing sugar.

Preheat the oven to 190°C/375°F/gas mark 5.

Put the egg yolks in a bowl and the whites in another bowl (this one needs to be completely clean and grease-free). Add half the granulated sugar to the yolks and, using an electric hand whisk, whisk on high speed until the mixture is thick, pale and fluffy, about 3–4 minutes.

Lower the speed, then pour in the vegetable oil, little by little, whisking all the time until it's mixed in. Pour in the cold water in a slow, steady stream, again whisking continuously. The mixture will be quite thin at this stage.

Sift the flour, baking powder and matcha powder over the mixture. Fold in gently with a spatula or large metal spoon until all the flour has been incorporated and the mixture is smooth. As the flour is added, the mixture will thicken considerably. Clean the beaters well.

Whisk the egg whites until soft peaks start to form, then add the remaining sugar and whisk until stiff peaks form, about 30–60 seconds.

Add a third of the egg white mixture to the matcha mixture and use a spatula to gently mix the two together, loosening the mixture slightly. Add half of the remaining egg white mixture and stir very gently to incorporate it all, then repeat.

Spoon the mixture evenly among the paper cases. Lift the muffin tray slightly off the work surface, then drop it back down to remove any excess air bubbles.

Bake on a low shelf for 15 minutes, until risen and firm to the touch. Leave to cool while still in the muffin tray.

Once the cakes are completely cool, take each one out of the muffin tray and peel away the paper case. Lift onto a flat serving plate and dust with matcha powder and icing sugar, if using. Serve with the mango.

デザート

DESSERTS

チーズケーキ　　　*JAPANESE CHEESE TARTS*

Makes
6

❋ FOR THE PASTRY

100g (3½oz/1 stick) unsalted butter,
　at room temperature, cut into small
　pieces
a pinch of salt
1 tsp granulated sugar
1 medium egg, beaten
160g (5½oz/1½ cups) plain flour,
　plus a little extra for rolling out

❋ FOR THE FILLING

120g (4½oz/½ cup) cream cheese, at
　room temperature
50g (2oz/¼ cup) granulated sugar
1 medium egg, beaten
125ml (4fl oz/½ cup) double cream
1½ tablespoons plain flour
2 tsp lemon juice

You'll also need six 9cm (3½in)
　tartlet tins.

Think mini cheesecakes, encased in a buttery pastry. The very subtle squeeze of lemon works a treat here – it's just enough to cut through the sweet, rich-tasting cream cheese filling.

Make the pastry. Put the butter into a large bowl and add the salt. Using an electric hand mixer, cream the butter and salt together until smooth. Add the sugar and continue to whisk until the mixture is pale.

Gradually add the beaten egg to the mixture, mixing well every time you add more. Use a spatula to scrape the mixture down from the sides of the bowl occasionally, and don't worry if the mix looks curdled.

Sift the flour into the bowl and use a spatula to cut and fold the mixture together, pressing it against the side of the bowl, too, until all the flour has been incorporated and the mixture forms a dough. Use your hands to gather it together and lightly knead together to make a smooth ball. Wrap in clingfilm and chill for 2 hours.

Cut the dough into 6 equal pieces. Take one piece and shape into a small, flat disc with your hands, so it is ready to roll out. Lightly dust a work surface or board with flour and roll out the disc out until it is big enough to line a tin. Place the dough on top of the tin and carefully lower it down into the sides. Use your fingers to press against it so it holds its shape. Cut or roll off any excess dough. If the tin is fluted, press the pastry into each flute with your fingers.

Prick the bottom of the pastry lightly with a fork. Repeat for the other 5 pieces of dough. Cover the tins with clingfilm and place in the fridge for 30 minutes.

Preheat the oven to 200°C/400°F/gas mark 6.

Take the tins out of the fridge, remove the clingfilm and lift onto a lipped baking tray. To bake blind, line each tin with a small round piece of baking parchment and fill with baking beans. Bake in the oven for 15 minutes.

When the pastry is slightly brown, remove the baking beans and put back in the oven for a further 5–6 minutes until the pastry is cooked and pale golden.

Take out of the oven and set aside to cool, still in their tins, while you prepare the filling. Lower the oven temperature to 190°C/375°F/gas mark 5.

To make the filling, put the cream cheese in a bowl and beat until smooth. Add the sugar and mix well. Add the egg and combine.

Pour in the cream and mix for 3–4 minutes until the mixture is like a thick batter. Sift the flour into the bowl and fold in lightly with a spatula. Stir in the lemon juice.

Spoon the mixture equally among the cooked pastry tart cases, making sure the tops are even (a small palette knife is helpful here).

Bake in the oven for 12 minutes, until the filling is set and still pale in colour. Cool in the tins for 15 minutes, then remove the tarts from their tins and cool further on a wire rack.

抹茶とピスタチオの
クッキー

GREEN TEA AND PISTACHIO COOKIES

75g (3oz/¾ cup) plain flour

20g (¾oz) kinako powder (see tip)

5g (⅛oz) matcha powder

50g (2oz/½ stick) unsalted butter, at room temperature

50g (2oz/¼ cup) golden caster sugar

1 medium egg yolk

10g (¼oz) shelled pistachios, chopped, plus 12 extra

10g (¼oz) cornflakes

25g (1oz) white chocolate, finely chopped

These bite-size biscuits feature cornflakes for crunchiness, pistachios and nuggets of white chocolate for sweetness. Lovely with after-dinner coffee, they also go well with the Matcha Ice Cream and Black Sesame Ice Cream.

Preheat the oven to 180°C/350°F/gas mark 4.

Put the flour, kinako powder and matcha powder in a bowl and mix together. Set aside.

Beat the butter in a separate bowl until it is soft and creamy. Add a third of the sugar and beat in, then do the same again twice more, until the mixture is smooth and creamy.

Add the egg yolk, a third at a time, and beat again after each addition until smooth.

Sift the flour mixture into the egg mixture and carefully fold together to combine. Add the chopped pistachios, cornflakes and white chocolate and fold in again.

Divide the mixture into 12 pieces and roll each into a ball. Place on a baking tray lined with greaseproof paper, leaving a 2cm (¾in) gap between each ball of dough.

Press each piece down with your hand to flatten and push a pistachio on top. Bake for 15 minutes or until the mixture looks pale golden brown around the edges.

Take out of the oven and transfer to a wire rack to cool. Store in an airtight tin for up to five days.

TIP

If you can't get hold of kinako powder, use ground almonds or oat flour instead.
You can also freeze the cookie dough, once shaped. Put on a baking sheet and bake from frozen for 15–20 minutes at the same temperature above.

黒ごまアイスクリーム　*BLACK SESAME ICE CREAM*

400ml (14fl oz/1¾ cups) whole milk

75g (3oz/⅓ cup) caster sugar

3 large egg yolks

2 tbsp honey

2 tbsp black sesame seeds, roasted and ground

3 tbsp neri goma (black sesame paste) or tahini

1 tsp vanilla extract

200ml (7fl oz/scant 1 cup) double or whipping cream

a pinch of salt

If you can't track down black sesame paste, you can still make this by swapping in the Middle Eastern sesame paste, tahini. It's a very good match in terms of flavour and the ice cream will still look the same once it's made.

Pour the milk into a small pan and bring to a simmer. Take the pan off the heat.

Whisk the sugar and egg yolks together in a heatproof bowl until the sugar dissolves and the mixture looks pale. Stir in the honey, ground sesame seeds and black sesame paste and whisk until well combined.

Slowly pour the hot milk into the sesame mixture in a slow and steady stream, stirring all the time.

Wash the saucepan quickly, then place it back on the heat and pour the mixture back into it. Heat over a low-medium heat, stirring all the time, until the custard thickens. If you have a thermometer, it should reach around 80°C/176°F. It's important not to let the mixture start to boil (or if you have a thermometer go any higher than 83°C/181°F) otherwise the egg will cook and scramble the mixture.

Take the pan off the heat immediately and pour the liquid into a large, shallow, heatproof sealable container – it'll cool quicker if it sits over a larger surface area. Once cool, stir in the vanilla. Cover and refrigerate.

Pour the cream into a bowl and whisk with the salt until the mixture has thickened and looks bubbly on top.

Carefully fold the whipped cream into the cold sesame milk mixture. Return to the fridge for 2–3 hours (or overnight) until completely cold.

Churn the mixture in your ice-cream maker, following the manufacturer's instructions, for around 25 minutes. Transfer to an airtight container and freeze for several hours before serving.

抹茶アイスクリーム *MATCHA ICE CREAM*

480ml (17fl oz/generous 2 cups)
whole milk
250ml (9fl oz/generous 1 cup) double
or whipping cream
100g (3½oz/scant ½ cup) caster
sugar
a pinch of salt
2–3 tbsp matcha powder, depending
on how strong you like it (see tip)

There are just five ingredients in this recipe. The creamy base is milk, cream and sugar heated together until just warm, then the matcha is whisked in, so it tastes a bit like a milky cream tea – and is very moreish. Pair with a Green Tea and Pistachio Cookie (see page 154).

In a saucepan, whisk together the milk, cream, sugar and salt.

Place the pan over a medium heat and stir. As the mixture begins to warm and bubbles appear around the edge, whisk in the matcha powder. Take care not to overheat otherwise the matcha powder will clump when it goes into the pan.

Continue to stir until it comes to the boil and starts to foam. Take the pan off the heat immediately and pour the liquid into a large, shallow, sealable heatproof container – it'll cool quicker if it sits over a larger surface area. Leave to cool, then chill for 2–3 hours until completely cold.

Just before churning, give the mixture a whisk again to help blend the granules that have settled in. Transfer to an ice-cream maker and churn according to the manufacturer's instructions, around 20–25 minutes.

Spoon into an airtight container and freeze for at least 3 hours before serving.

TIP

If you can't get hold of matcha powder, use green tea instead and infuse the cream with it. You'll need around 8 tablespoons, cut from tea bags, and use in place of the matcha powder. Once the cream comes to the bubble, whisk in the tea. Then set the pan aside for 5 minutes so the tea infuses into the cream, then strain into the container.

CHAPTER 8

✳

A GUIDE TO
SAKE

ご馳走様でした

gochisousamadeshita

—

A polite expression used after finishing a meal.

A GUIDE TO SAKE

Sake is an important part of life and culture in Japan and has been for thousands of years. It is complex in flavour, primarily made by fermenting rice, and boasts a long and well-founded reputation for excellence and consistency that extends far beyond the country of Japan. With its rich variety of tastes, flavours and aroma, sake makes a great accompaniment to food, regardless of cuisine, cooking style or ingredients, as well as a profoundly satisfying drink to enjoy on its own.

RAW INGREDIENTS

Sake is made primarily from three main ingredients; rice, water and koji (the magical healthy fungus responsible for fermentation). Its production process has many parallels with wine and beer, but it has a much more complex and labour-intensive brewing process.

RICE – *SAKAMAI*

Like grapes, there are dozens of rice varieties, but only those varieties officially classified *sakamai* may be used in the production of sake. These styles of brewing rice have a very large grain that is roughly 25 per cent larger than table rice; their stalks grow much taller and they are harvested much later than table rice. The country of Japan is divided into 47 Prefectures, or districts, and certain ones have developed a reputation for growing specific types of *sakamai*. There are over 60 classified *sakamai*.

RICE POLISHING

The outer layers of the rice kernel are high in proteins and vitamins while the centre is rich with starch. While the outer layers are good for consumption, they are not good for sake production so, before the koji can be used, the outer layers of the rice grain have to be milled or polished away. This process is similar to stripping beans in coffee production. The ratio of rice remaining is called the *seimai buai* (rice-polishing ratio).

WHITE HEART
Rich in starch content and low in minerals.

OUTER LAYER
Rich in proteins and vitamins.

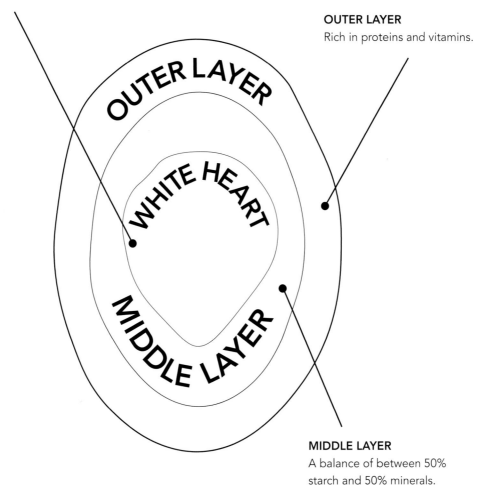

MIDDLE LAYER
A balance of between 50%
starch and 50% minerals.

Sake is graded on its rice-polishing ratio, with the higher grade sakes being made with higher polished rice. As you can see from the diagram above, the white heart of the rice grain occupies about 50 per cent of the kernel. Sake made with rice polished to at least 50 per cent is considered to be the best type of sake for this reason.

KOJI

Wine was probably mankind's first achievement in making alcohol. Because most fruits are full of sugar it is only necessary to apply the yeast which naturally exists in the skin to create alcohol. However the process is more difficult with ingredients like grain and rice because of their lack of sugar. However, these ingredients have an abundance of starch and this can be converted into sugar. In sake making, koji (*Aspergillus oryzae*) is the magical ingredient that makes this happen. Koji is basically a naturally occurring fungus that produces enzymes as it grows and performs a similar role to malt in beer-making. It is these enzymes that turn the starch into sugar through a process called saccharification. There are three different colours of koji, but it is the yellow type that we are most concerned with in sake making. Originally invented for brewing sake, it produces a crisp and fruity aroma.

WATER

Sake is almost 80 per cent water and this means the quality of the water has a huge influence on the final product. Sake breweries will usually use a nearby naturally occurring river or mountain stream or even hot-spring to source their water. Most water comes from deep underground. The most common type of water in sake making is *fushimizu*, found in a part of Kyoto, and considered to be one of the purest, but sake is made across Japan with many regional variances.

   The hardness of the water is also a very important factor. In general, Japanese water levels are at the very soft end of the scale and soft water is best suited for sake production.

SPECIAL SAKE GRADES

Over time, by adapting certain stages of the brewing process, breweries have been able to engineer special grades of sake. Here are just a few of these grades – new ones are being developed all the time.

NIGORI (cloudy or milky): Sake which is filtered, then the milky sediment is returned to the sake through a mesh to give an opaque or cloudy appearance, hence its name.

NAMA: Unpasteurised sake. Sake is usually pasteurised twice, but Nama sake foregoes one or both of these pasteurisations. The result is a delicate sake that must be kept chilled and consumed soon after opening, but which has a unique taste profile.

YAMAHAI/KIMOTO TSUKURI: Sake made with one of the more traditionally made yeast starters *(natural koji)*. The end product is usually earthier.

TARU: Sake that has been stored in casks and is therefore characterised by its refreshing taste and the wooden aroma of Japanese cedar.

GENSHU: Sake where not as much water or even no water is added to dilute the sake at the end of the production process resulting in a stronger taste. Sake is naturally produced at 18–19% ABV, giving it the highest naturally occurring alcohol content of any brewed beverage. Most sake is then diluted to the 15–16% ABV level.

MUROKA: Sake that does not undergo any filtering, producing a more earthy and complex flavour.

KOSHU/AGED SAKE: Sake that has been aged in either oak or cedar wood casks for between 5–15 years.

ORIZAKE: The sake lees *(the sediment)* are left in the finished product to add a yeasty flavour similar to 'sur lie' in Muscadet production.

HAPPOSHU (sparkling sake): This type of sake has a second fermentation stage which produces natural gas, like champagne, and puts this in the sparkling wine category.

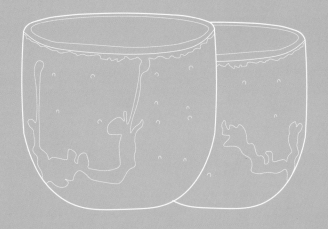

Afterword
by the **Marine Stewardship Council**

Our oceans are in crisis, but that does not mean we need to stop eating seafood. From climate change to plastic pollution to overfishing, the threats to oceans and the life within it are serious. Yet, there are reasons to be optimistic. As people grow more aware of these threats, so too has the willingness to work together to find global solutions. There is huge momentum behind this collective effort, including a United Nations goal on conserving and sustaining our oceans.

One way to be part of that momentum is to look for the Marine Stewardship Council blue label. MSC certified fish, seafood and seaweed comes from scientifically sustainable stock in well-managed fisheries that minimise their wider environmental impact. Across the world thousands of products are certified to the MSC standard, rewarding hundreds of fisheries for operating sustainably. This is essential for healthy oceans.

This cookbook is a fantastic celebration of Japanese cuisine. All of us can enjoy these recipes without jeopardising fish and seafood stocks for this and future generations by using ingredients with the MSC blue fish label. This will help to ensure we can continue eating much-loved Japanese seafood dishes now and in the future.

Acknowledgements

To Jacques Attal and Laurent Boukobza – those early pioneers who brought hand-crafted, quality sushi to retail environments internationally, making good Japanese cuisine accessible to millions across the globe.

To Remy, Doungporn, Henry, Lynn, Khraisri and all of those skilled chefs who contributed recipes from Sushi Gourmet, Genji, Mai, Wok St, Sushi Market, Sushi Kano, Sushi & Robata, Poké-Lélé and our University of Sushi.

To Juliette, Denise and other passionate foodies who have worked tirelessly to bring Japanese food to life.

To the many amazing passionate Japanese food suppliers, our partners in True World and Tazaki.

To Michael, for teaching me kanji whilst we studied sake production together and helping to craft the sake guide.

To Emma Marsden, for taking my rough notes and transcripts in various forms and transforming them into simple, neat and workable recipes, for her huge enthusiasm for the task and for jumping in with many of our chefs, and for the way she rolls!

To Howard Shooter's camera and Max Antoine's pen in photography and illustration that fill these pages and capture the essence of *itadakimasu* and *Japanese Cooking for the Soul*.

To Albert and Michel Roux Jr, Jean-Louis Taillebaud, Gaston Lenotre, Pierre Koffman and many other legendary culinary luminaries whom I have worked with over the past four decades and who have inspired me and given me passion for great food and life.

Jason Lalande d'Anciger
Managing Director, Hana Group UK & Ireland

ABOUT HANA

Hana Group is winning the hearts and minds of customers as the trend for healthy food and in-store theatre explodes, revolutionising the way we shop.

The Hana Group UK & Ireland brands consist of Sushi Gourmet, Genji, Mai, Wok St, Sushi Market, University of Sushi, Poke-Lele, Sushi & Robata and Izakaya.

Hana Group UK & Ireland has been awarded 'Great Taste' (2019), 'Grocer New Product' (Winner 2019) and 'Quality Food Awards' accolades, winning best overall product in the UK over thousands of entries (Gold Winner Food To Go 2017, 2018, 2019).

Hana Group UK also picked up 'Best New Business Awards 2019' Business of the Year and Overall Winner. FSB Start Up Business of the Year 2018, UKBA 'Dons' Gold Award 2019 for innovation and more.

The recipes have been inspired by talented chefs from some of this country's favourite and award-winning Japanese eateries including Sushi Gourmet, Mai, Genji, Sushi Market, University of Sushi, Sushi Kano, Sushi & Robata, Poké-Lélé and Wok St.

Black Sesame Ice Cream

Chicken Teriyaki Salad

Green Temptation

Grilled Tofu Skewers with Spicy Peanut Sauce

Matcha Ice Cream

Original Ramen

Salmon Teriyaki Salad

Secret Garden Rolls

Spicy Miso Ramen

Tofu Nigiri

Tofu Teriyaki Salad

Vegetable Tempura with Toasted Sesame Seeds

Wasabi Ebi

Cristal Salmon Rolls

Green Tea and Pistachio Cookies

Prawn and Mango Crystal Rolls

Seafood Teppanyaki

Teppanyaki Duck

Tofu and Spinach Gyoza

POKÉ LÉLÉ

Hilo Poke

Honolulu Poke

Pacific Poke

Beef and Coriander Shumai

Grilled Salmon in Balsamic Onion Glaze

Gyoza Wrappers

Mango Tango Rolls

Salt and Pepper Baby Squid

Sesame-grilled Asparagus Rafts

Soft Shell Crab Tempura

Tofu and Chilli Tempura

Tofu and Quinoa Shumai

SUSHI **GOURMET**

Avocado Maki

Chicken Katsu Noodles

Chicken Poke

Classic Meat Gyozas

Classic Stir-fried Rice

Cucumber Maki

Gyu Yaki – Japanese Beef Skewers

Prawn Gyoza

Prawn Tempura with Spring Onions

Salmon Temptation

Spicy Prawn Tempura Rolls

Stir-fried Noodles with Tofu

Stir-fried Rice with Chicken

Stir-fried Rice with Vegetables

Tuna Crunch Rolls

Veggie Crunch Rolls

Yakitori Chicken Skewers

SUSHI KANO

Crunchy Rice Salmon Tartare

Double Salmon Roll

Salmon Crunch Rolls

SUSHI MARKET

Beef Teppanyaki

Luxury Calamari Rolls

Mixed Vegetable Curry

Salmon and Tuna Sushi

Spinach Gyoza Wrappers

Beef Ramen

Chicken Ramen

Spring Rolls

Tofu Wok Bowl

Vegetarian Noodle Bowl

Cherry Roll Cake

Chicken and Cucumber Crystal Rolls

Green Tea Chiffon Cakes

Japanese Cheese Tarts

Japanese Custard Puddings

Pork and Cabbage Gyozas

Salmon and Avocado Crystal Rolls

Vegetable Ramen

INDEX